Volume 8, Issue 3 September 2004

Femme Fatale

Special Issue
Edited by Valerie Steele

Fashion Theory

The Journal of Dress, Body & Culture

Fashion Theory: The Journal of Dress, Body & Culture

Editor
Dr. Valerie Steele
Director
The Museum at the Fashion Institute of Technology, E201
Seventh Avenue at 27th Street
New York, NY 10001-5992
USA
Fax: +1 212 924 3958
e-mail: valerie@fashiontheory.com

Book Reviews Editor
Christopher Breward
Research Department
Victoria and Albert Museum
South Kensington
London SW7 2RL

Exhibitions Reviews Editor
Alexandra Palmer
Royal Ontario Museum
100 Queen's Park, Toronto
Ontario M5S 2C6, Canada
Fax: +1 416 586 5877
e-mail: alexp@rom.on.ca

Please send all books for review to the Book Reviews Editor

Aims and Scope
The importance of studying the body as a site for the deployment of discourses is well-established in a number of disciplines. By contrast, the study of fashion has, until recently, suffered from a lack of critical analysis. Increasingly, however, scholars have recognized the cultural significance of self-fashioning, including not only clothing but also such body alterations as tattooing and piercing. *Fashion Theory* takes as its starting point a definition of "fashion" as the cultural construction of the embodied identity. It aims to provide an interdisciplinary forum for the rigorous analysis of cultural phenomena ranging from footbinding to fashion advertising.

Anyone wishing to submit an article, interview, or a book, film or exhibition review for possible publication in this journal should contact Valerie Steele (at the address listed to the left) or the Editorial Department at Berg (1st Floor, Angel Court, 81 St Clements Street, Oxford, OX4 1AW, UK; e-mail: enquiry@bergpublishers.com).

Notes for Contributors can be found at the back of the journal.

© 2004 Berg. All rights reserved. No part of this publication may be reproduced or utilized in any form or by any means, electronic or mechanical, including photocopying and recording, or by any information storage or retrieval system, without permission in writing from the Publisher.

ISSN: 1362-704X
www.fashiontheory.com

Ordering Information   Four issues per volume.   One volume per annum.   2004: Volume 8

By mail:	Customer Services Turpin Distribution Ltd Blackhorse Road Letchworth Hertfordshire SG6 1HN UK	By fax:	+44 (0) 1462 483011
		By telephone:	+44 (0) 1462 672555
		By e-mail:	subscriptions@turpinltd.com

Free online subscription for print subscribers. Full color images available online. Access your electronic subscription through www.ingenta.com or www.ingentaselect.com

Inquiries   Editorial: Kathryn Earle, Managing Editor, e-mail: kearle@berg1.demon.co.uk

Production: Ian Critchley, e-mail: icritchley@bergpublishers.com

Advertising + subscriptions: enquiry@bergpublishers.com

Subscription Rates: Institutional base list subscription price: £105.00, US$168.00.   Individuals' subscription price: £40.00, US$65.00.

Reprints of Individual Articles   Copies of individual articles may be obtained from the Publishers at the appropriate fees. Write to: Berg, 1st Floor, Angel Court, 81 St Clements Street, Oxford, OX4 1AW, UK.   Printed in the United Kingdom. SEPTEMBER 2004

Indexed by the International Bibliography of Social Sciences; The MLA International Bibliography; Sociological Abstracts; ARTbibliographies; H.W. Wilson Company Art Index and Abstracts and the Anthropological Index Online (AIO), the Royal Anthropological Institute of Great Britain and Ireland.

⊛ BERG

Page 267

Page 301

Page 315

Page 329

Page 335

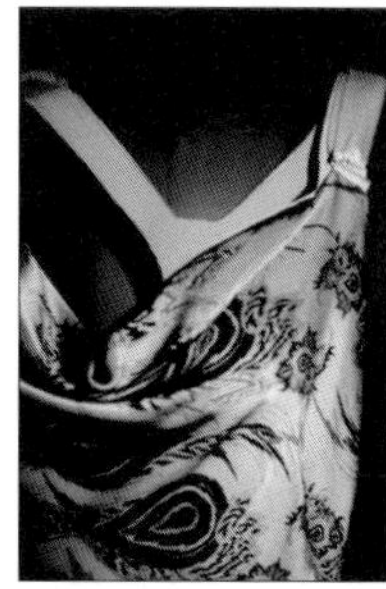

Page 339

Contents

Editor
Dr. Valerie Steele
Director
The Museum at the Fashion
 Institute of Technology, E201
Seventh Avenue at 27th Street
New York, NY 10001-5992
USA

Fax +1 212 924 3958
e-mail: valerie@fashiontheory.com

249 **Letter from the Editor**
Valerie Steele

251 **Weaponizing the *Femme Fatale*: Rachilde's Lethal
Amazon, *La Marquise de Sade***
Emily Apter

267 **Fashion and the White Savage in the Parisian Music
Hall**
Rae Beth Gordon

301 **L'Allure de Chanel: The Couturière as Literary
Character**
Lourdes Font

315 ***Femme Fatale*: Fashion and Visual Culture in
Fin-de-siècle Paris**
Valerie Steele

329 **Exhibition Review**
Manolo Blahnik—A Retrospective
Janice West

335 **Exhibition Review**
Fashion & Textile Museum, London
Amy de la Haye

339 **New Gallery Review**
"What Happened to all those Lovely Costumes?"
Amy de la Haye and Rebecca Quinton

351 **Book Review**
Through the Wardrobe
Valerie Wilson Trower

355 **Book Review**
Fashion Classics from Carlyle to Barthes
Julia Pine

359 **Book Review**
Couture and Commerce
Nicola White

363 **Book Review**
Dangerous Designs
Emma Tarlo

367 **Book Review**
Yeholee: Work
Nicolas Cambridge

Fashion Theory, Volume 8, Issue 3, pp. 249–250

Letter from the Editor

The Museum at the Fashion Institute of Technology held its first annual fashion symposium in January, 2003, in conjunction with the exhibition, *Femme Fatale: Fashion and Visual Culture in Fin-de-Siècle Paris*. The following year, the second annual fashion symposium was held in conjunction with the exhibition, *Fashioning the Modern Woman: The Art of the Couturière, 1919–1939*. The speakers included a number of brilliant and famous scholars—from Emily Apter to Eugen Weber. Curators and other museum professionals also presented papers. Betty Kirke, for example, received a standing ovation for her presentation on Madeleine Vionnet, the great couturière who has been the subject of her life's work.

This issue of *Fashion Theory* includes three essays based on papers presented at the first symposium and one from the second symposium. It would have been gratifying to include all of the papers presented, but a number had already been published in other forms. Mary Louise Roberts, for example, spoke to great acclaim at both symposia, but readers can easily find her books, *Disruptive Acts* and *Civilization Without Sexes*. Similarly, Dilys Blum's lecture on Schiaparelli was drawn from her recent exhibition catalogue. Inevitably, some conference papers work most effectively as a performance with visuals, and need to be substantially rewritten in order to function as an essay. This was certainly the case with my own essay on the *Femme Fatale* exhibition. It is entirely possible, indeed likely, that future issues of *Fashion Theory* will include additional essays drawn from the second symposium.

Rae Beth Gordon caused a great sensation at the first symposium with her paper on "The White Savage in the Parisian Music Hall." Readers will also be fascinated by the material that she has uncovered, although, regrettably, they will not be able to see the extraordinary film clip that she played. Emily Apter, whose work I have found so stimulating, enthralled the audience with her paper on "The Weaponized Woman," which analyzed the role of fashion in the work of the fin-de-siècle decadent novelist, Rachilde. Indeed, several members of the audience subsequently told me that they had ordered copies of Rachilde's novel, *Monsieur Venus*. Lourdes Font's essay on Chanel was presented at the second symposium, within the context of a number of papers focusing on individual female fashion designers, including Jeanne Lanvin, Elsa Schiaparelli, and Madeleine Vionnet. Amy de la Haye also spoke on Chanel, while I discussed the entire regiment of women who dominated Paris fashion in the 1920s and 1930s. Yet Chanel was in many respects unique, and Font's essay throws light on why we find her so endlessly fascinating.

The third annual fashion symposium in February, 2005 will be on the subject of *Glamour: Film, Fashion, Fantasy*. Stay tuned.

Yours sincerely,

Valerie Steele

Fashion Theory, Volume 8, Issue 3, pp. 251–266
Reprints available directly from the Publishers.
Photocopying permitted by licence only.
© 2004 Berg. Printed in the United Kingdom.

Weaponizing the *Femme Fatale*: Rachilde's Lethal Amazon, *La Marquise de Sade*

Emily Apter

Emily Apter is Professor of French and Comparative Literature at New York University. She is the author of *Feminizing the Fetish: Psychoanalysis and Narrative Obsession in Nineteenth-Century France* (Cornell, 1991) and most recently *Continental Drift: From National Characters to Virtual Subjects*, (Chicago, 1999).

In Rachilde's *La Marquise de Sade*, a quintessential French decadent novel published in 1887, a mock tournament is staged by a locally stationed regiment to rally patriotism on the eve of the Franco-Prussian War. Presiding over the entertainment is the novel's central character Mary Barbe, a hussar's daughter, cast as the "spirit of war" in a costume ordered from a Paris couturier. She wears: "a violet and white silk gown, a silver breastplate enhanced with brilliant glass beading, a silver helmet set with little golden eagles" and wields a tapering lance. Described in the local newspaper, the dress, "draped Greek-style on one side, revealed a body tunic of dark violet silk brocaded with gold cameos; the silver-mail buskin came down as far as the cameos while the panels of the skirt fell very long and full at the back, showing off the somewhat unformed hipline of the adolescent. The breastplate perfectly clasped her frail bosom, enlarging what was too frail and her neck emerged naked from a coil of false rubies as from a bucket of blood."[1]

The lines of the dress record that transitional moment in fashion history when the *belle époque* taste for swollen bust lines and full hips gives way to a desire for the more androgynous allure of Grecian turn-of-the-century styles. This is of course, the costume of a female warrior, and in describing the dress Rachilde exhibited the expertise of a seasoned fashion writer. Though she by no means invented the Amazon—a type that traces back to the female warriors of Asia Minor in ancient times, famous for their prowess in battle, their female-only socius, their propensity for killing male progeny, and for slicing off one breast as mark of allegiance—she certainly gave her an original, period-hybridized uniform, matching the Greek tunic with medieval armor. The costume is embellished with a necklace of red rubies, worn like a wound that has become a prize jewel, and set off against the violet color of the dress. The choice of purple was clearly of importance to Rachilde, who, according to her executor Romana Severini Brunori, "always wore violet or mauve." ("A propos de mode, Rachilde s'habillait toujours en couleur violette ou mauve, c'était sa couleur privilégiée!" she wrote to me recently in a letter.) Violet and mauve were famous decadent hues; the palette of choice for Proust's courtesan Odette, as well as the mascot of literary partisans of the "violet quill" who gathered around Oscar Wilde.[2] In this instance, though, violet is coded as a darker shade of blood emblematic of the blood-sucking proclivities of a new breed of *femme fatale*, the Vampire-Warrior.

Rejected by her father for not being a boy, the heroine Mary Barbe pursues a life-long vendetta against men, killing her baby brother, her uncle, her husband, and her lover.

Structured as a kind of psychoanalytic "case study" of female vampirism, or *Bildungsroman* of female sadism, the narrative traces how Mary becomes addicted to blood after witnessing the slaughter of an ox whose vital fluid will be used to provide her ailing mother with a fortifying cocktail. At the time, it was not uncommon to prescribe a glass of blood as a remedy for tubercular symptoms. But in the novel this prophylactic justification is stripped away, laying bare the thin veneer that separates civilization from barbarism. Blood sacrifice in a French abattoir appears as a pagan ritual marking the loss of innocence and the birth of unhealthy appetites for blood and war. Thereafter, Mary will be obsessed by a taste for blood, envying her father's access to scenes of carnage as he departs for the front of the Franco-Prussian War. As she matures she develops a taste for the morgue, naturalist novels, wax museums, the exploits of spiritists, lesbian bars, and specialty houses. In Rome, premier site of imperial decadence, she savors the spectacle of a lovers' quarrel that ends with a bloody knife. Back in Paris, she frequents the demimonde milieu of transvestite subculture at the bal Bullier and dreams of attaching one of these beautiful young men to her bed with satin ribbons while stabbing him to death with hairpins. At the end of the novel, we find her returned to the meat-packing district delighting in the spectacle of butcher boys performing riffs while drinking ox blood. Mary raises a glass and, drunk on the odors of soon to be slaughtered flesh, dreams "of the murder of one of those fallen males which she would carry out with a heart serene and a dagger raised" (MS 279).

This final image of Mary, dagger in hand, poised to strike, places her in a long line of lethal *femmes fatales*. In her book *Lethal Love: Feminist Literary Readings of Biblical Love Stories* Mieke Bal offers a provocative interpretation of the Samson and Delilah legend (emphasizing its endurance as a paradigm of woman's wickedness, seduction, unfaithfulness, treason), that emphasizes the myriad ways in which the "fatality" of the *femme fatale* was construed to cover a gamut of fears and phobias, from lustmord to castration anxiety. Noting that the Hebrew word for "master" can also be used to denote rape, she implies that Delilah's attempt to suborn Samson by extracting the secret location of his strength is tantamount symbolically to female rape, a fatal assault on masculine power.[3] In the Bible, in answer to Delilah's insistent query about the source of his power Samson replies: "If they bind me with seven fresh bowstrings not yet dry, then I shall become weak as any other man."[4] Caught in the bowstrings of his own language, he is rendered captive. This idea of enslavement is clearly foreshadowed in Camille Saint-Saens's opera libretto in which Delilah sings: "He is my slave: To gratify my hate,/my power to ensnare him!/I want him, overcome by love,/to be humbled in his turn!" Psychic bondage merges with the fin-de-siècle fear of succumbing to fatal illness. When *Samson*, after losing his hair, his strength, his sight, and his honor in the eyes of the Israelites laments: "Alas, I defiled love in giving it to this woman," we have what amounts to a medical version of morbid love, an allusion to the well-founded fear of syphilis that afflicted a huge proportion of the French populace. As premier symptom of cultural decadence the *femme fatale* was demonized as a carrier of poisoned germs and spiritual bankruptcy, fostering the link-up of misogyny to an evolutionist, world-historical sense of fatality. Max Nordau, the Spengler of the *fin de siècle*, wrote in his best-selling book *Degeneration* of the decline of civilization; the "formlessness" of historical reality as history cedes to the hallucinations and apocalyptic visions of a drugged, hyperstimulated mass culture. Technology and the burgeoning society of spectacle lead, in his view to crass commercialism, a worship of beauty robbed of moral idealism, and a fascination with perverse, non-reproductive sexualities that glorify an aesthetics of sterility. Central to this aesthetics of sterility was the *femme fatale*, the high priestess of *l'art pour l'art*, standing before the mirror, a figure of narcissism, artifice, autoeroticism, and non-reproductive sexuality, a prime culprit in the downward spiral of the natality rate. Delilah, Empress Theodora, Cleopatra, Judith, Semiramis, Thaïs, these biblical and historical egeria were arraigned alongside latter-day examples of dangerous women, both real and imagined.[5] They included Eugène Delacroix's 1831 painting of a bare-breasted woman in the allegorical role of "Victory Leading the People," Thérèse Figueur, one of the rare female soldiers in Napoleon's army who fought in all the major campaigns; Louise Michel, the *pétroleuse* of the barricades; and Madeleine Pelletier, the suffragette, Bizet's Carmen, and Zola's destructive courtesan Nana, burning through the fortunes of her suitors, much like her real-life counterpart Liane de Pougy, rumored to have ruined her aristocratic lover by exacting colossal sums for the privilege of viewing her naked for a single night.

In the seemingly endless serial production of *femmes fatales*, catering to the seemingly bottomless appetite for their consumption on the part of the *fin-de-siècle* public, no character reigned more supreme than Salomé, immortalized in J. K. Huysmans's *A Rebours* (published three years prior to *La Marquise* in 1884):

> A pensive, solemn, almost august expression on her face, she begins the lubricious dance which is to awaken the slumbering senses of the ageing Herod; her breasts rise and fall, their nipples hardening under the friction of her whirling necklaces, her belts, her rings, flash and sparkle; on her triumphal gown—pearl-seamed, silver-flowered, gold-spangled—the breastplate of jewelry, each of its links a precious stone, bursts into flame, sending out sinuous, intersecting jets of fire, moving over the lustreless flesh, the tea-rose skin, like a swarm of splendid insects whose dazzling wing-sheaths are marbled with carmine, spotted with saffron yellow, dappled with steely blue, striped with peacock green.[6]

Huysmans's prose rendition of the lapidary facture of Gustave Moreau's painting may well have served Rachilde as a source of inspiration for Mary Barbe's engagement dress: "I want the dress to be the color of suffering" she announces to her stunned dressmaker (MS 184). What she obtains is a garment of emerald green satin, a velvet laced bodice spangled with bronze mesh (another coat of mail), whose purple and blue reflections connote insect wings, as well as the black and blue bruises to be inflicted on her future husband and lovers. Every decorative element in the dress is a piece of weaponry: "the bodice was high-cut yet it opened with an unexpected plunge between the breasts" (think sword or dagger). The bodice left her hips as if naked, and all down the folds of the very clinging skirt ran flowerless rose branches studded with thorns" (MS 185). This is a get-up that not only hurts, it kills, as we see from the hair ornament that sets off the dress; consisting of a dead bird (described as a "poor massacred creature"), pierced by a dull metal pin (MS 185). Having vowed to remain aloof from men, even if she concedes to marriage, Mary Barbe— the name itself is a weapon—uses her "rebarbative" gown to declare war on the male sex.

If I have chosen to dwell on the theme of clothing that kills, it is in the conviction that by weaponizing the *femme fatale* Rachilde not only literalizes the well-worn cliché that women "arm" themselves as seductresses with the help of an "arsenal" of beauty secrets, she also reads the *femme fatale* as a figure of war, whose fashion and self-fashioning derive directly from the historical conditions of the Franco-Prussian War. Indeed, I would submit that *La Marquise de Sade*, while not generally classified as an 1870 war novel at all, should be placed squarely in a tradition that includes Guy de Maupassant's "Boule-de-suif" (in *Les Soirées de Médan*, 1880), and antiwar manifesto "La Guerre" (published in 1881 in *Le Gaulois*), Abel Hermant's notorious 1886 antiwar narrative *Le Cavalier Miserey* (which satirized the feminized French soldier), and Emile Zola's 1892 epic *La Débâcle*. *La Débâcle* locates the root cause of decadence in the corruption and complacency of Napoleon III's Second Empire, and glorifies the homosocial bonding of soldiers on the battlefield. By contrast, *La Marquise de Sade* presents male virility in a sorry state; the primary reason for military defeat, and a sign of the ascendancy of women. Mary's strength grows in inverse proportion to the diminution of male national energies: "Blood was draining from French veins," so the narrative goes, "and Paris, heart of the world, no longer beat the drum for distant wars" (MS 269). Only Guy de Maupassant in works such as "Boule-de-suif" (1880), "Mademoiselle Fifi" (1882), or his 1884 short story "Le Lit 29" comes close to Rachilde in assigning a woman pride of place in a war narrative. In "Boule-de-suif," the courtesan Elisabeth Rousset, a loyal patriot, attempts valiantly to hold out against the Prussian invaders, only to be coerced by her fellow travelers—a band of bourgeois and aristocratic refugees—into yielding to their lascivious desires. After partaking of her food, and profiting from her sexual sacrifice, these collaborationists, lacking all compunction, impugn her character. Such a display of rank hypocrisy becomes itself the sign of what Maupassant would characterize as "the great debacle of a people accustomed to military victory."[7] Failed by their own army, the citizens of France "survive" by colluding in the violation of their own.

This plot line is reprised in "Le Lit 29" when the mistress of a French soldier contracts syphilis after being raped by Prussian soldiers, she performs a "patriotic" duty by infecting as many of the enemy as possible before succumbing to the disease. The callous French soldiers misrecognize her sacrifice and dismiss her as a whore of the Prussians, but the story's moral diegesis points its finger at the culpability of the French army. Irma's dying words—"You, with your cross of honor, you have not have done as much as I have! I merit it far more than you, more than you do, I tell you, for I have killed far more Prussians than you have!"—convey the message that France might have won the war had women been at the helm.[8]

La Marquise de Sade develops a similar "Joan of Arc of the sex trade" theme—but where Maupassant creates a *femme fatale* doubly victimized by the Prussians and her French compatriots, whose fatality resides in her transmission of infectious disease, Rachilde tenders an avenging angel, a personification of *la Revanche* whose fatality is part and parcel of her militant character. As "une fille de militaire," like Rachilde herself, Mary Barbe is genetically wired to become a woman warrior. As we know from Rachilde's memoir *Quand j'étais jeune*, the character of Colonel Daniel Barbe was modeled after her own father, an officer in the Algerian campaign of 1845–9, a veteran of 1870, and a violent man born out of wedlock, rejected by his mother and reared in an orphanage. The novel's picaresque is informed by the nomadic life of military troops disruptively setting up camp in local communities. Mary's upbringing in various garrison towns becomes the basic training of an Amazon. However, in Rachilde's edition of the Amazon, the stereotype of the *femme fatale* favored by *fin-de-siècle* male authors is singularly lethal. Whereas the *femme fatale* seeks narcissistic gratification in seducing and subjugating men, Rachilde's woman warrior is differently motivated. Her crimes (which include whipping, mutilating, poisoning, biting and branding), are cast as acts of courage, spurred by an ethical (dare we say feminist?) imperative to right the wrongs historically committed against the weaker sex; as well as by her patriotic commitment to redeeming the reputation of France in the wake of humiliating defeat.

Ascribing a *revanchiste* motivation to the *femme fatale*, Rachilde evolved an idiosyncratic form of militarist feminist militance, combining images of the female soldier (typified by the period's caricatures of "les Amazones de la Seine," a battalion of women deployed for the first time in the war of 1870), a strain of anti-Republican intransigent royalism espoused by her family, and an erotic radicalism all her own.[9] This erotic radicalism forms an interesting contrast to the "erotic militance" of her rival Colette. Judith Thurman has suggested that what erotic militance signified for Colette was a "revolt against any normative standards for desire, and against all sentimentality in the carnal domain."[10] The heroism of the sex worker, or of the woman skilled at faking orgasm to shore up the ego of a weak man; the courage to experiment with the unconventional ménage (*partouzes*, the Lolita complexes, arrangements between older women and gigolos); the social dangers incurred by pursuing same-sex love; the choice of solitary self-sufficiency over marriage (as in *La Vagabonde*), these were the practices defining Colette's idea of militance. But where Colette confined herself to sexual politics in art and life, Rachilde mobilized eroticism in the service of nationalism, in effect, superimposing an epic of gender war on the genre of the war novel and re-staging the defeat of 1870 in the key of a feminist revenge tragedy.

Born in Périgord in 1860, Marguerite Eymery, who later took the pen name Rachilde, died at the ripe age of ninety-three in 1953. Her life span thus covered, as Melanie Hawthorne has noted, three Franco-German conflicts. "One of the most significant events of Rachilde's childhood," Hawthorne writes, "was also an event of national and international importance . . . although she would experience World Wars I and II more directly, arguably it was the Franco-Prussian conflict that caused the most long-term disruptions in her life, the national crisis of 1870–71 mirrored a personal, familial one."[11] War and fashion, commonly situated, as diametric opposites, the one associated with the bellicose world of the father, the other with the domestic sphere of the mother, emerge as the two poles anchoring Rachilde's early writing. Having begun her career as a fashion columnist (under the pseudonym Madame de Sauves) for journals such as *L'Opinion*, *Le Henri IV*, and *L'Echo de la Dordogne*,— a fact which helps explain the proficiency and prevalence of fashion descriptions in her novels—it comes as little surprise that her first published work, *Monsieur de la Nouveauté* (which appeared in 1880) takes the fashion floor for its *mise en scène*. As one of the earliest department store novels, *Monsieur de la Nouveauté* might be said to have "scooped" Emile Zola's far more celebrated *Au Bonheur des dames* by some three years. According to Claude Dauphiné, this story of a young man of peasant stock who comes to the city and meets his ruin at the hands of a fickle *modiste* soon after he is hired as a sales clerk by the *grand magasin* "le Grand Roi," was read at the time as a warning against allowing men to infiltrate the frivolous world of feminine fashion. As its title suggests, the novel set up a pattern of reversed gender roles that Rachilde would consistently rework in her best-known fiction, especially *Monsieur Vénus* (1884), *La Marquise de Sade* (1887), and *Madame Adonis* (1888).

If fashion were Rachilde's inaugural theme, military culture was the dominant topos of the second novel, *La Femme du 199e Régiment* published in 1881.[12] Introducing a conceit that would be redeployed in *La Marquise de Sade*, the novel features officers with farcical names like Corporal Chiendunum and Captain Botteferme obsessed with the nocturnal visits of a mysterious "personne du sexe."[13] The purposefully ambiguous gender of this "person of sex" anticipates Rachilde's ruthless satire of "gays in the military" in *La Marquise de Sade* through the personage of Captain Corcette, who, it is rumored, "made his start as a handsome calvary officer in the dressing room of a famous general" (MS 151).

Fashion and war are entwined in virtually all of Rachilde's subsequent novels. *La Marquise de Sade* begins with the desecration of a dress. Mary's virginal white dress, worn as she accompanies her aunt to the slaughterhouse, is sprayed with the blood of the sacrificed ox, a thinly transparent symbolization of a pagan rite or a wartime sacrifice, but also of deflowering (with sexual initiation conflated with instantiation of taste for blood and murderous revenge). In *Monsieur Vénus* (1884) fashion sets the engine of the text in motion (along with the theme of gender inversion and transvestism), since the reason for the heroine's sortie is her need for an evening gown for a costume ball. She enters the shop of a fabric flower maker only to discover a male rather than a female dressmaker. His sister is ill, Jacques Silvert informs her, "for the time being, I am Marie Silvert."[14]

This first impression of her future love-slave captures him working on a garland of "very big roses of flesh-colored satin with deep red, velvety tracings. They ran up his legs to his shoulders and around his neck." (MV 174–5). The flowers feminize him, clothe him in drag, but they are also like ropes that threaten to choke him to death. Their first conversation is about fashion: "You see, Monsieur, it is for a costume ball, and I am in the habit of wearing flowers especially designed for me. I will go as a water nymph in a Grévin costume wearing a tunic of white cashmere with green beads and rushes; so you see, there must be a background of river plants, nympheas, sagittaria, lentils, water lilies. . ." (MV 276). The nymphea in symbolist literature and impressionist painting was coded as a decadent flower. Grafted from the eastern lotus, it was thought to emit a deadly aphrodisiac odor sending lovers into extreme paroxysms. Raoule's flowered dress, though apparently an innocent concoction, proves to be as sinister as her "long black dress with a long tortuous train" that she wears on her second meeting with Jacques. On her hand she sports "a big cameo ring mounted on two lion's claws. When she caught Jacques's hand, again she scratched him. In spite of himself a sensation of terror overcame him. The creature was a devil" (MV 287). Here, fashion and the woman are as one; united in a single, violent intent. The same conceit prevails in *La Jongleuse [The Juggler]* published in 1900, where it becomes difficult to determine whether the dress—referred to as "a queen"—commands the wearer or the reverse.

> This woman let her dress trail behind her like a queen trailing her life. She left the brightly lit hall, taking with her its darkness, draped by a thick shadow, by an air of impenetrable mystery that came right up to her neck and clasped it as though to strangle her. She took small steps, and the tail of black, full, supple material fanned out, rolled a wave around her, undulated, forming the same moiré circles that are seen in deep water in the evening, after a body has fallen.[15]

Intimations of murder by strangulation, suffocation, and drowning are worked into the garment, and there is a pronounced militaristic menace in the style of her hair:

> and what showed above her funereal envelope seemed very artificial: a painted doll's face, decorated with a bonnet of smooth, shining hair with steely glints, hair that stuck to the temples, too twisted, too fine, so fine it seemed like imitation silk, a shred of her black dress, that satiny, almost metallic, sheath. With such a tight hairstyle set above thin red ears that seemed literally to bleed under the weight of a sharp-edged helmet, she was whiter with her makeup than any other made-up woman. (J 4)

Readers of the time may have been well acquainted with the artifice of deluxe courtesans and Baudelairean flowers of evil, but Eliante Donalger's helmet-head of steel and sharp edges announces a new class of *femme fatale*—the *guerillère-garçonne*—one no longer committed to acquitting France of national disgrace, but devoted single-mindedly to waging gender war. Short hair and cross-dressing may thus be added to the accouterments of the *femme fatale* as preferred weapons of choice in a crusade to usurp the privileges of masculinity.

Raoule de Vénérande, heroine of *Monsieur Vénus*, makes love to her ephebe while sporting a menswear evening suit, complete with black patent leather pumps and a white silk waistcoat. Remaining clothed, she undoes the waistcoat, exposing one naked breast. The nipple is described as a "closed flower bud that was never to blossom into the sublime pleasure of giving milk," underscoring the resolute masculinism of the Amazon, whose article of faith and communal bond rests on renunciation of child-bearing (MV 354). This image of a single-breasted, male-attired dominatrix not only updates the Amazon to turn-of-the-century codes, it reinforces the use of cross-dressing in the battle of the sexes.

There were of course plentiful examples of real-life cross-dressers to be inspired by in nineteenth- and early twentieth-century France: among them, the writer George Sand, the painter Rosa Bonheur, the actress Sarah Bernhardt, the horsewoman La Marquise de Morny (a lesbian aristocrat who performed a scandalous pantomime with Colette wearing male drag and who was legendary in her taste for debauch, was thought to have been the model for la Mary Barbe), the traveler and convert to Islam Isabelle Eberhardt, Colette, Romaine Brooks, Una Troubridge, and the photographer Claude Cahun. Impetus for the masculine turn in women's dress also came from within the fashion industry: from equestrian style, the outfits devised for women in sport, the theatrical period clothes commonly worn at masked balls, the costumes donned by actresses playing male roles (Sarah Bernhardt in the part of Lorenzaccio or Hamlet), and the sartorial travesties assumed by women courting each other in the guise of young boys (as when Natalie Clifford Barney played the page during her seduction of Liane de Pougy).

Rachilde herself was renowned for cross-dressing well before the Colette and Barney circles made it the imprimatur of the Parisian city of women. Victor Margueritte, author of the immensely influential best-seller *La Garçonne*, published in 1922, was an early admirer of Rachilde's and was reputed to have used her as a model for the flapper. She applied for and received official permission to wear masculine attire in 1884 and apparently did so for ten years. And yet, what cross-dressing actually signified for her at the turn of the century remains somewhat ambiguous. In a chapter on "La Mode" in her 1927 polemic *Pourquoi je ne suis pas féministe* Rachilde insisted that her principal reason for dressing in men's clothing was pecuniary—a men's suit lasted longer, did not show dirt, and provided an original *tournure* for a *femme de lettres* who was expected by the public to set a trend or reinforce her reputation with a particular way of dressing.[16] But the issue was obviously more complex; as Melanie Hawthorne reminds us, cross-dressing "remains an imprecise term. It can refer to aspects of transsexual or transgender practice . . . or it can mean gender bending . . . One kind of performance aims to avoid attention, the other to attract it" (H 109). Hawthorne emphasizes how Rachilde experimented with an amalgam of masculine and feminine details of style. In a series of publicity shots dating from around 1895, she had herself photographed in a *tailleur* that "highlights the feminine through the exaggeration of fabrics (brocades, embroidery, ribbons) "but which is offset by masculine tailoring and a man's hat. (H 147–8). This motif of the men's fedora resurfaced in an engraving of Rachilde by Langlois (probably based on the photographic series) that graced the cover of the 1887 issue of the mass-circulation magazine *La Vie Moderne*, the same year in which *La Marquise de Sade* appeared. Rachilde's hair was a topic of gossip; rumor had it that she had sold her locks to a Russian count as a rebuff to his advances. In the Langlois engraving, her hair does appear to be short, though Hawthorne allows that it may just be been pinned back.

Whatever the true story, Rachilde clearly took great pains to present herself to the public as a masculine woman, an extension of her fictional avatars. In *Monsieur Vénus* Raoule dresses for her wedding as a warrior maiden, in a silver brocade, swansdown jacket. When one of the party remarks that it looks as if she has had her hair cut short, Raoule, overhearing, acknowledges that it is "a recent fashion that I have purposefully adopted" (MV 348). With her skills at fencing, her self-portrait as Louis XV with a riding crop, her revolver, and her animal skins, Raoule deploys gender reversal as the ultimate psychic bludgeon with which to vanquish masculinity. "A strange life began for Raoule de Vénérande, from the fatal moment when Jacques Silvert gave up his power as a lover and became hers to do with as she would, a lifeless object who let himself be loved, because his own love was powerless" (MV 312). "I am in love like a man with a man, not a woman" (MV 303), Raoule confesses, thus identifying herself as a gay-identified woman (for Jacques, it turns out, has a weakness for her suitor the Baron de Raittolbe). Exemplifying what Terry Castle has called "cross-homosexual love" Jacques attempts to seduce the Baron while masquerading as "Madame Silvert."[17] Meanwhile Raoule, the "real" Madame Silvert, arrives at the Baron's apartment masquerading as Monsieur Silvert. Overcoming the remonstrations of the valet, she bursts into the room and discovers an aroused Raittolbe threatening to shoot himself if he proves unable to surmount his homosexual panic. Raoule repossesses her feminine garments, and exits as "Madame Silvert," her hair astonishing the valet in its transition from gold to black. Raoule's conjugal charade clearly registers as double drag, for her role as "wife" is far more of a masquerade than her cross-dressed persona as "husband" of a feminized man. Having entirely usurped the place of the man, Raoule orchestrates a gay suicide, condemning Jacques and the Baron to a fatal duel. The objective of gender war is thus achieved—death to the male race! *La Marquise de Sade* pursues a similar end, by allowing the heroine to appropriate the male prerogative of not bearing children. On the night of her marriage, Mary Barbe informs her stupefied spouse that she holds men in horror and has no intention of giving him an heir ("Je ne veux pas être mère") (MS 215). Quickly she evolves into an erotic torture artist, a cold and indifferent mistress who beguiles her husband into signing away his fortune to her in a moment of distracted frenzy. He desires her "because she is like no other woman," because she is a monster who hurts him. Having molded him into the perfect male masochist, Mary weaponizes psychic cross-dressing in the service of masculine extinction.

By the end of *La Marquise de Sade* such imperilled masculinity announces the death throes of civilization: "Deep down, she felt that decency and sanctity are marvels, and would have wanted a country like the heroic France of old, while neither Stock Exchange nor Morgue were a meeting place for every class. But, since she did not aspire to the lofty height of chargé d'affaires for the Creator, with a mixture of ennui and disdain, she left the Seine to flow on, its waters clogged by decomposing warriors who had battled on to suicide" (MS 271–2). Here we find evidence of Rachilde's ideological suasion, at once decadent and antidemocratic. For Mary's monarchist hatred for the leveling of social classes ushered in by the Third Republic, enlists her "patriotically" in the execution of sexual crimes that will hasten the demise of republican institutions. Moreover, the reference to "decomposing warriors who had battled on to suicide," which applies the language of the war hero to social outcasts who have drowned themselves in the Seine, suggests that, in like manner, France after the 1870 debacle has embarked on a course of national suicide.

Defeatism and sexual decadence were consistently paired as double symptoms of fin-de-sièclism in Rachilde's fiction. In a late novel published in 1921 titled *Les Rageac* (a compound term blending rage and political reaction), the plot of *La Marquise de Sade* is reprised but with greater autobiographical fidelity. Once again, the heroine is the daughter of an army officer; an Amazon-in-the-making nicknamed "Magui," whose habit of putting her hands behind her back when standing up to her mother brings to mind "a miniature of Napoleon."[18] And once again, we find fashion mobilized as a tool of combat. Madame Rageac's couturier devises a costume whose seductive frills and military emblems are guaranteed to charm the Emperor into granting her husband clemency. (Captain Rageac has been imprisoned for fighting a duel.) She dons a short dress of "Metternich green" emblazoned with the legend "Follow me young man" and worn over "boots à *Souvarow*," so-named in honor of a famed Cossack general of the 1790s. Like all other seductresses in Rachilde's novels, violet is the color of choice. Madame Rageac swathes her body in an extravagant purple velvet coat, with a majestic train and fur mantle. The strategy of the coat does not succeed however, first, because it suggests that Madame de Rageac would rival the empress in wearing sumptuous court attire, and second, because it is covered with dead animals, thereby offending her righteous daughter Magui who is a staunch advocate of animal rights. Magui's conversation with the dressmaker concerns the little black tails that still seem to wag against the white background of the fur. "They are the beasts themselves, the ermines" the dressmaker answers. "And were they killed on purpose to put them there?" the girl wonders, to which the seamstress replies: "Naturally, we couldn't exactly sew them on alive." This revelation arouses a superstitious horror in the "mini-Bonaparte," who vows secretly to strangle as many princesses as there are black tails on the train of the coat. As in *La Marquise de Sade*, fashion is the goad to murder.

The genre of family melodrama gives way to the genre of the war novel in Part II of *Les Rageac*. Titled "Notebook of an officer of 1870," it draws on Joseph Eymery's actual war diary. With its precise notations of provisions, rations, instructions for the care of arms, specifications for dress code on the battlefield, deprivations (the absence of salt and meat), medical remedies (put ground rice in the coffee against dysentery), and sober accounting of the dead and wounded, the journal offers a documentary view of the sordid particulars of everyday life on the front lines while charting the downward spiral of the campaign after the disastrous battle of Metz. Captured yet unwilling to surrender his arms, Captain Rageac is made a prisoner of war. From his cell, he writes to his wife, more exercised about the capitulation of the Third Republic, which he sees as the mouthpiece for an ideology of defeatism, than about the miserable condition of his health (R 138). In the same breath, he laments that he has a daughter instead of a son, a refrain of paternal misogyny that shows a broken army man fatally underestimating the powers of female militarism to restore the honor of France.

The trope of a female Napoleon continues in the heroine's determination to fight against the lot of women, particularly the intractable injustices of the marriage market. In Part III of *Les Rageac* Captain Rageac engages in pitched battle with his spouse over the fate of their daughter. The captain counsels his chosen suitor to wage his marriage campaign "as you would have in 70 under fire from the enemy" (R 235). To counter this onslaught, Magui resorts to the tactics of the *femme fatale*, attending a masked ball disguised as her own great-grandmother, a Marquise guillotined during the Revolution. Channeling the spirit of a powerful ancestor, she intimidates her suitor with the redoubtable spectrality of a revenant, blinding his vision with glints from her metallic headdress. The return of the dead Marquise also plays as a return of Rachilde's own novel *La Marquise de Sade*, a text summoned back from the *fin de siècle* to haunt the twentieth-century novel.

Like her notorious characters, Rachilde herself gained notoriety as a weaponized woman. In 1925 she was reputed to have brandished a revolver while attending a literary banquet at the Closerie de Lilas in honor of Saint-Pol Roux. According to accounts by those present, Rachilde entered into a terrible altercation with André Breton, who had taken issue with her Germanophobia after she had responded "no!" to a poll asking whether French women should be allowed to marry German men. Breton, keen to defend his German friend Max Ernst, called her "une fille à soldats" (a soldier's slut). Amidst surrealist cries of "Long Live Germany" and "Down with France," Rachilde was hustled along at age sixty-eight to the police station.[19] Her anti-Prussian chauvinism attracted ridicule from the surrealist generation, who seemed to have missed the surreal production values of this spectacle of a gun-toting *petite vieille* threatening to fire a socially destabilizing "coup" in defense of an abstract idea. By all measure, Rachilde should have been a surrealist icon, lionized like the anarchist "poet" of terror, Ravachol, the revolver-wielding Alfred Jarry (dubbed "the perfect anarchist" by Breton), or the parricidal Violette Nozières, lauded by the surrealists as a "poet of crime."[20]

Rachilde may have enjoyed a measure of literary celebrity in her own time as the inventor of uniquely decadent heroines embodying a militarist ascription of decadent aesthetics, but her reputation was on the wane by the early 1920s; her persona ripe for becoming the fodder of a surrealist joke. Reread today, however, Rachilde's oeuvre seems astonishingly germane; a veritable source-book of avatars of the female militant. The idea of the weaponized woman conjures up in contemporary history images of female suicide bombers with explosives strapped to their bodies and a fanatical cause in their hearts. If these images seem remote from the turn-of-the-century *femme fatale* who used the artifice of seduction to vanquish the will of the stronger sex, they appear less distant when a text like *La Marquise de Sade* is read as the war novel which it truly is, albeit a very particular kind of war novel, but a war novel nonetheless, in which gender war and war between nations are deeply imbricated. Rachilde's text alerts us to the way in which the specter of the female warrior—or latter-day Joan of Arc—continues to be adduced as a sign of social decadence and political decline, even as it points to how gender war continues to be enfolded into "real" war, whether in the form of controversies surrounding women in the military, or in the form of justification for intervention abroad (the liberation of women in Afghanistan and Iraq). These are anachronistic interpretations of course, but they attest to subliminal messages stored in the period costumes of the *fin de siècle* that have yet to be fully appreciated. For lurking in the folds of the hyper-sexualized fashions of the *femme fatale*—the slashed fronts, pinched corsetry, bulging bustles, and mawkish ornamentation of dead birds and frozen nature—lies not the malleable coquette, but the weaponized woman, ready for battle in the bedroom and on the front. As courtesan couture gradually makes room for masculine riding habits and the sexless uniform of the Amazon, the weapons of choice shift with the fashion. Cross-dressing—emblem of the denaturalization of femininity—delivers its deadly blow to ideologies of the state and the family. Shepherded along by Rachilde, a new look of feminist militance comes into focus, bringing in its train the dawning of twenty-first-century gender wars.

Notes

1. Rachilde (1994). Further references to this translation will be to this edition and will be denoted in the text as "MS."
2. For a history of the color mauve see Garfield (2001).
3. See Bal (1987).
4. *The New English Bible* (16:7) cited by Bal (1987: 52).
5. For a discussion of feminist personification of historic legendary character-types see "Metropolitan Masquerades" in Apter (1999).
6. See Huysmans (1977) and the English edition translated by Baldick (1959: 45).
7. See de Maupassant (1974: 84).
8. See de Maupassant (1979: 183).
9. For a discussion of the "Amazons of the Seine" see Clayson (2002).
10. See Thurman (2000: viii).
11. See Hawthorne (2001). Further references to this work will be denoted in the text as "H."
12. I have been unable to track down a copy of this work and base my description of it on the one offered by Claude Dauphiné (1995).
13. In leaving the gender of the "person of sex" unspecified, Rachilde points ahead to her overt treatment of "gays in the military" through the personnage of Captain Corcette in *The Marquise de Sade*.
14. Rachilde (1998: 275). Further references to this translation will be to this translation and will be denoted in the text as "MV."
15. Rachilde (1990: 3). Further references to this translation will be denoted in the text as "J."
16. See Rachilde (1927).
17. See Castle (1996).
18. *Les Rageac* (1921). Further references to this work will be denoted in the text as "R."
19. See Léauteaud (1954–66: 60–8).
20. See Breton *et al.* (1933).

References

Apter, Emily. 1999. *Continental Drift: From National Characters to Virtual Subjects*. Chicago, IL: University of Chicago Press.

Bal, Mieke. 1987. *Lethal Love: Feminist Literary Readings of Biblical Love Stories*. Bloomington, IN: Indiana University Press.

Baldick, Robert (trans.). 1959. *Against Nature*. New York: Penguin.

Breton, André *et al.*, 1933. *Violette Nozières*. Brussels: Editions Nicolas Flamel.

Castle, Terry. 1996. *Noel Coward and Radclyffe Hall: Kindred Spirits*. New York: Columbia University Press.

Clayson, Hollis. 2002. *Paris in Despair: Art and Everyday Life under Seige (1870–71)*. Chicago, IL: University of Chicago Press.

Dauphiné, Claude. 1995. *Rachilde: Femme de Lettres, 1900*. Périgueux: Pierre Fanlac.

de Maupassant, Guy. 1974. "Boule de Suif." In Louis Forrestier (ed.) *Contes et nouvelles*, vol. 1. Paris: Gallimard.

de Maupassant, Guy. 1979. "Le Lit 29." In *Maupassant: Contes et nouvelles*. Paris: Gallimard.

Garfield, Simon. 2001. *Mauve*. New York: W. W. Norton.

Hawthorne, Melanie C. 2001. *Rachilde and the French Women's Authorship. From Decadence to Modernism*. Lincoln, NE: University of Nebraska Press.

Huysmans, Joris-Karl. 1977. *A rebours*. Marc Fumaroli (ed.). Paris: Gallimard.

Léauteaud, Paul. 1954–88. *Journal Littéraire*, vol. V. Paris: Gallimard.

Les Rageac. 1921. Paris: Flammarion.

Rachilde. 1927. *Pourquoi je ne suis pas féministe*. Paris: Aux Editions de France.

——. 1990. *The Juggler*. Trans. Melanie C. Hawthorne. New Brunswick, NJ: Rutgers University Press.

——. 1994. *The Marquise de Sade*, pp. 155–6. Trans. Liz Heron. Sawtree: Dedalus.

——. 1998. "Monsieur Vénus." Trans. Madeleine Boyd. In Asti Hustvedt (ed.). *The Decadent Reader*. New York: Zone Books.

Thurman, Judith. 2000. "Introduction." In Herma Briffault (trans.) *The Pure and the Impure*. New York: New York Review of Books.

Fashion Theory, Volume 8, Issue 3, pp. 267–300
Reprints available directly from the Publishers.
Photocopying permitted by licence only.

Fashion and the White Savage in the Parisian Music Hall

Rae Beth Gordon

Rae Beth Gordon is Professor of French and Comparative Literature at the University of Connecticut. In addition to numerous essays on medicine, literature, and aesthetics, she has written *Ornament, Fantasy and Desire in 19th-Century French Literature* (Princeton University Press, 1992) and *Why the French Love Jerry Lewis: From Cabaret to Early Cinema* (Stanford University Press, 2001).

Every time that the Belgian artist Félicien Rops came to Paris, he was astonished by the fantastical look of the contemporary Parisian woman, "who seemed to come from another world, *as foreign as a Hottentot*."[1] That was in 1866; thirty years later, the primitive look is satirically portrayed infiltrating high fashion (Figure 1). As Valerie Steele has pointed out, to be a fashionable woman was to blur the lines between the *femme du monde* and the demi-monde of cocottes. "Courtesans and actresses in fin-de-siècle Paris were instrumental in launching new and overtly erotic fashions, which were rapidly adopted by respectable women around the world" (Steele 2003: 2). Some of the most well-known cocottes were singers in the café-concert. The hallmarks of the look made fashionable

Figure 1
Lucien Métivet, "Civilisation!"
Le Rire, 23 January 1897.
Courtesy BnF (Bibliothèque
nationale de France)

by the *femmes fatales* of the music hall and café-concert included an ostentatious display of jewelry, feathers, a daring décolleté, and a very prominent derrière. The distance between them and the Hottentot was not as far as one might think. Yet, more than vestimentary practice, I want to analyze a constellation of bodily practices in the setting of the music hall which heralded the fashion for the savage. In fact, it is fair to say that the image of the *savage*—so often emphasized in the way people saw cancan dancers, semi-nude chorus girls, and the singers discussed in this article—was in fact the *predominant* figure of the sexually desirable woman in the last quarter of the nineteenth-century and in the beginning of the twentieth. And for that reason, it also made up part of the image of the fashionable Parisienne.

Some of the *femmes fatales* who appeared on the Parisian music-hall stage[2] were celebrated courtesans or notorious for other reasons. Among them were la Belle Otero, Liane de Pougy, Casque d'Or,[3] and Mata Hari. Both Otero and Mata Hari were famous for their exotic dancing, the scandalous belly dance having first enthralled spectators at the 1889 Exposition Universelle, with the vogue for Spanish dancing following close behind. Jules Lemaître wrote, "the horrors of the belly dance revealed to me the decency of the can-can" (in Ducrey 1996: 269). Lemaître, whose article is entitled "The Legacy of the Exposition [Universelle]," continues: "thus the dance of the Orient is invading us, and that is why I do not fear sounding the alert, not as a moralist . . . but as a good Occidental . . . This invasion, if it continues, would be deplorable. Our dance is so superior to the other one by its grace, by its wit, by its decency! [The two forms of dance] truly express two different and even contrary souls, two races, two civilizations" (in Ducrey 1996: 263). Exotic dances—whether they "invade" France from the Orient, from Spain, from sub-Saharan Africa, or from black America—bring with them a pronounced fear of contagion: contagion of the low and the bestial. Caroline Otero, who danced the fandango and became one of the most famous courtesans of the *belle époque*, was described as "a beautiful beast. A magnificent wild animal in whom instinct governs all" (Lanoux 1957: 181). This article focuses on a performer who also began her career with Spanish and Oriental dances: Colette's intimate friend, Polaire, one of the biggest stars of turn-of-the-century Paris. Her celebrity was founded in great part on her association with the forms of the Low that we will have occasion to consider here. That did not prevent Polaire from becoming a fashion icon of the *belle époque*, on the contrary. Jean Cocteau said of her: "Polaire dominates fashion: she unsettles women. She inspires a nervous irritation in men" (Cocteau 1935: 90–1).[4] Cocteau's observation is not without import for the androgynous mystique that Polaire projected and to which I will return at the end of this article. The adoption of African clothing and ornament, as implied in the Figure 1, like the adoption of African movements and gesture, as we will see, often brings with it an aura of virility.

Polaire, along with Mistinguett, rose to stardom as an Epileptic Singer, a genre that was created in 1875. A close look at Polaire will reveal an underlying association with racial stereotypes, an important, but now lost, component of her appeal . . . an association with not only African women who were exhibited in Paris in the nineteenth century, with not only photographs and drawings of African women that appeared in popular, middlebrow, and highbrow magazines, but also with black American entertainers beginning with touring minstrel shows and culminating in the explosion of a new dance rage in 1902: the Cake-Walk. I begin, then, with Polaire's predecessors and fellow Epileptic Singers, as well as with the African dancers who shared the spotlight in the same period.

Epileptic Singers and the Fashion for Sex, Comedy, and Ugliness

As I wrote in my book, *Why the French Love Jerry Lewis*, "the irresistible pull of fashion, of modernity, governed the café-concert public, and nothing was more modern, more fashionable between 1880 and 1900 than nervous pathology, whose jerky rhythms and movements define popular song and performance style in the period" (Gordon 2000a: 80). Songs like "Nervous," "Too Nervous," "Tata's Tic," "I'm a Neurasthenic," and "La Parisienne épileptique" were sung by Epileptic Singers. Muguette de Trévy, for example, sang: "I'm a nervous little woman. In reality, the blood of a turnip runs through my veins, but today *le grand chic* is to appear *neurasthénique*." As though to confirm the truth in these song lyrics, Edmond de Goncourt wrote in his *Journal* on April 17 1889 that "Society women today look just like hysterics from the Salpêtrière" (Goncourt 1957) vol iv, page 961. André Chadourne wrote in 1889 that "the public is thirsty for these songs . . . it can't get enough. And cases of pathology like this are met with more often than one would think" (Chadourne 1889: 277). These performers, along with many others in the last quarter of the nineteenth century in France, modeled their performance style on the tics, grimaces, contortions, and convulsive movements and gestures of epileptics and hysterics. Thanks to phenomenal media attention on hysteria, the great majority of spectators recognized this source. The extraordinary popularity of Epileptic Singers and Idiot Comics exactly coincided with the startling upsurge of cases of hysteria in Parisian hospitals, feeding into and capitalizing on a cultural phenomenon which was just getting under way. It is not by chance that the style fell out of fashion in France around 1907–08, that is to say, at around the same time that Charcot's convulsive, spectacular version of hysteria was supplanted by that of Babinski and others.[5] The journalist Georges Montorgueil (1893: 2) gave one a good idea of what excited the Parisian public in the 1890s when he wrote, "A good half of today's hit songs . . . belong to the late Dr. Charcot's home for the agitated. They jerk and tremble. They have gesticulatory hysteria." In its restructuring of the body, hysteria became a cultural phenomenon and created a new form of expression in the arts. More precisely, the theme of hysteria in popular entertainment produced a novel form of spectacle. Contained in the unpretentious but nonetheless extraordinary modernity of this new form of spectacle were the seeds of Dada and surrealism.

The *chanteuse épileptique* created a style of sexual lewdness combined with clowning, corporeal contortions, and grimaces: the creation of a female grotesque, to use Mary Russo's term. Montorgueil (1893: 3–4) wrote that they were "so stupefying, so unexpected! And what clown-like poses!" Some even adopted the clown's hairstyle with a point at the top, the same hairstyle that could also be seen on minstrels performing in Paris. This marriage of the erotic, the pathological, and the comical

Figure 2
"Eugénie Fougère"
Iconography dossier Per 9996
"Eugénie Fougère," BnF, Dép't
des Arts du spectacle.
Courtesy BnF

was an entirely new female persona. Just how fashionable was this comical yet sexy figure? This article will show that the attraction these traits held, extending even to a delight in ugliness, was at the heart of the popularity both of black entertainers and of the Epileptic Singers. Thanks in part to the posters and drawings of Jules Chéret, Willette, and Widhopff, where the tamed-down, purely *seductive* aspect of the image was represented, the *chanteuse épileptique* came close to epitomizing la Parisienne. In this article, I want to show that under the frothy white petticoats there was more than a little of darkest Africa (Figures 2–4).

For the last quarter of the century, the *chanteuse épileptique* was one of the biggest draws in Parisian night-life.[6] The genre was created by Emilie Bécat at the Ambassadeurs in the summer of 1875. For the novelist, J.-K. Huysmans, Mlle Bécat is "that epileptic doll bleating and twisting her hips in those inept convulsions that made her a quasi-celebrity." Huysmans goes on to describe singers who remind him of La Bécat: they hold out their "paws" in front of them "that bob up and down like the imbecilic paws of porcelain monkeys" (Huysmans 1975: 227). Characterizations of this genre of singer as animalistic will become more and more frequent.[7] Emilie Bécat's convulsive gestures and leaps were described by Paulus, the most popular male singer of the 1870s and 1880s: "quicksilver seemed to run through her veins; she ran, she bounded, twisted herself with suggestive gestures [in] a short dress that showed off her calves completely. The public ate her up!" (Paulus 1908: 214). Mlle Bécat's costume as well as her epileptic movements would be imitated by a host of scantily clothed young women with small voices and big hopes.

When Violette came on stage at the Eldorado café-concert in the 1880s, the audience yelled, "'Take off your undies! . . .' '[Raise your skirt] higher! . . .' 'Let's see it!'" (Guilbert 1927: 149). "With the contortions

Figure 3
Poster, "Polaire aux
Ambassadeurs." Courtesy BnF

of a strangling chicken, a woman . . . bleated out a popular song" (Renault
and Le Rouge 1899: 116). In the following descriptions of the acts of
Epileptic Singers in the 1880s and 1890s, when the style was at its peak,
I have emphasized parallels with descriptions of Africans and black
Americans in the same period:

> Valentine Valti has "*big nostrils* . . . and bends over backward,
> shockingly, spreading her thighs, . . . *décolletée on top and dé-cul-
> otée* (cul = ass) on the bottom, with her gigantic hats, the star who
> has a good laugh" (*Courrier Français* April 5 1891: 8).

> Vanoni has a "*bizarre and charming* way of executing diverse
> dances" (*Courrier Français* January 10 1886); "Performing at the

Mlle Duclerc, dans la " Revue Déshabillée ", au Concert des Ambassadeurs
Reproduction de son affiche par A. Guillaume

Ambassadeurs, [she] is "half-singer, half-dancer, always ready to leap. . . . *With the chic of a Parisienne and the furious grace of the American*, this unleashed Fury [in her] gymnastic pantomime, is *The Agitated One* (*Courrier Français* June 7 1891).

Bonnaire joyfully "treated her breasts *like fetishes*, honoring them in [all her] songs, poses, and gestures." (Montorgueil 1893: 5; the word fetish here would necessarily have evoked contemporary exhibits of Africans in Paris. My emphasis in all citations.)

Mistinguett (who was as popular as Josephine Baker for over half a century in France) began as a *chanteuse épileptique*, "making gestures with . . . wild abandon" and comically shaking her arms, legs, and hair (Mistinguett 1954: 20). By 1899, she was a star at the Eldorado, singing "La Parisienne épileptique." She abandoned the style in 1907. "I was tired of the daily epilepsy, of sitting on the prompter's box, the better to gesticulate" (p. 41). "She seemed to symbolize the café-concert at its most modern, most frenzied, most fanciful"[8]. The "nervous" gommeuse, Foscolo, "was not afraid . . . *to be ridiculous, to make herself ugly.*"[9] Ugliness made singers distinctive and gave them great physical presence. Despite the décolleté, the lavish display of undergarments, and the sexual content of the songs, the erotic appeal of some of the singers and dancers is, as we see, at best a curious one.[10]

At the Casino de Paris, the very select public enjoys the cancan dancers headed by Nini-Pattes-en-l'air (Nini-Paws-in-the-Air). "Nini has wagered on an exhibition that is the funniest in terms of ugliness."[11] "Even her foot grimaces: "The little heel above her head points an ironic grimace" (Arthur Symons cited in Ducrey 1996: 282). "Mlle Abdala, taking advantage of her exceptionally skinny physique, made the grimace into an art form." Montorgeuil (1893: 17) wrote that Mlle Abdala was "ahead of her time." Not only was she "a rascally parody of woman, . . . she uses her charm to make herself ugly," but if one day, singers decide to exploit "a particular ugliness in the manner of Black musicians and dancers, then Mlle Abdala will be a star of the first magnitude." In fact, black minstrels and the black-face genre dubbed "Les Exotiques" were becoming so popular with audiences that the journalist predicted they might one day triumph and singers disappear. Montorgueil's assessment would prove to be right on the money, as will become clear when we discover how eagerly white musical singers seized on the association with blackness that became part of their aura.

Hysterical convulsions were confused with epilepsy, and still referred to as hystero-epilepsy because of the first stage of the attack, the "epileptoid," long after Charcot had distinguished the two nervous illnesses. Charcot labeled the second stage, the "clownesque," because of its acrobatic contortions. Among other common symptoms were contractures of the hands and facial asymmetry. Compare this photograph a of patient published in the 1878 *Photographic Iconography of the Salpêtrière* (Bourneville and Regnard) with Degas's 1877–8 lithographs, *Mlle Bécat aux Ambassadeurs* which show the singer very clearly reproducing a hysterical contracture of both hands (Figure 5).

The curious mixture of contorted corporeal poses, comical grimaces, and unabashed sexuality in lyric, movement, and dress may be difficult to understand today. It had certainly never been seen before on stage. However, if the combination of grotesque comedy and eroticism was new to the stage, the very same mix existed in the hysterical attacks of a great many female patients at the Salpêtrière Hospital. An 1878 case history

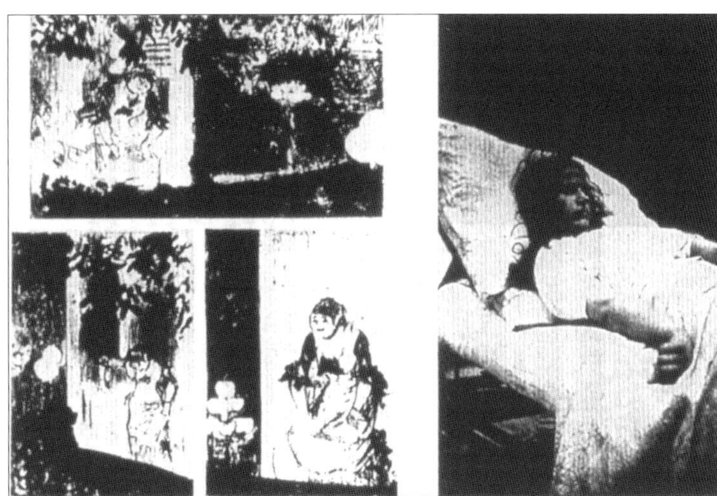

Figure 5

Degas *Mlle Bécat aux Ambassadeurs*, lithograph 1876–77. Courtesy Museum of Fine Arts, Boston. Gift of G.P. Gardner. / "Hysterical patient," *Iconographie de la Salpêtrière*, Vol. II, 1878. Courtesy Countway Medical Library, Harvard University.

of a hysteric with chorea describes her curious attack: "The face grimaces horribly, . . . then begins the habitual jolts and shaking. . . . Finally, she suffers a fit of manic agitation where she laughs without reason, gesticulates, jumps and dances" (Bourneville and Regnard 1878).[12] Dancing itself was far from being considered an innocent corporeal expression[13] and, in the 1870s, alienists insisted on the relationship of dance to hysteria. Dr Paul-Max Simon (1877: 98) wrote that "one put one's nervous system in unison with the jiggling and stamping of the music of Offenbach, and one invariably became hysterical and sometimes insane."

A year after Dr Simon published this startling observation (certainly hyperbolic, but which fit nineteenth-century theories of unconscious imitation seamlessly), Parisians were exposed to several strange new dance exhibitions. The year 1878 was a capital one for dance and concerns about contagion: it was the year of the first Exposition Universelle that showcased an African village with African dancing; it was the year that Zulus first danced on music-hall stages at the Folies-Bergère; it saw the first crest of popularity of the Epileptic Singer, and it was the second year of publication of the *Iconographie photographique de la Salpêtrière* with its case observations of chorea.

Concurrently with the appearance of minstrels in France, beginning in 1877, large numbers of Parisians flocked to the Jardin d'Acclimatation to see the African Villages, a scientifically endorsed ethnological exhibit.[14] It's important to note that exotic animals in captivity were displayed alongside these exotic beings who drew crowds precisely because they were so different. The way they looked, dressed, and lived appeared so extraordinarily uncivilized to Parisians that the juxtaposition with wild animals seemed to signal their status somewhere between animal and human being. To add to the thrill of this spectacle, mating rituals and cannibalism were also mimed as the "attraction" of the ethnological exhibits. Initially sanctioned as scientific, they became more and more theatrical and commercialized. Wild animals were not the only unflattering juxtaposition. "Monsters" —dwarfs and giants—were also exhibited at the Jardin d'Acclimatation in 1909. They had already been popular acts in the café-concert for some time, along with hunchbacked singers and emaciated comics, all grouped together in a genre known as Phenomena (*Les Phénomènes*), akin to freaks. Georges Montorgueil's portrayal of Mademoiselle Abdala came very close to classifying her as a Phenomenon but, as we saw, the journalist instead linked her to black entertainers. In fact, Africans—and by extension black Americans—were already associated with Phenomena, as the exhibition of the Hottentot Venus had already demonstrated at the beginning of the century. The attraction of the physically different was paramount in nineteenth-century entertainment, and in the latter part of the century, these attractions were tied to the fears surrounding degeneration and to Darwin's theory of evolution. Naturalists and physical anthropologists were eager to uncover simian characteristics in Africans, as illustrated by Cuvier's 1817 report published in the *Mémoires du Muséum*, a year after the dissection of the body of Sartjie Bartmann, "The Hottentot Venus." In addition to the extraordinary popularity of the "ethnological exhibits," crowds came in droves to the 1878, 1889, and 1900 Expositions Universelles to see the natives of the Congo, Dahomey, and Senegal perform their songs and dances.

Thus, highly sexualized savages and cannibals populated the imaginations of the French people in the 1880s through the first decade of the twentieth century. A journalist in the magazine *Fantasio* writes that "In Africa, lascivious dances to barbaric rhythms accompany the meeting of the sexes . . . Certain black women here and there are cannibals. But their charm is only heightened by it, from what one says . . ."[15] Posters foregrounding the bare-breasted Amazon warriors of Dahomey served to advertise the hugely successful play at the Théâtre de la Porte Saint-Martin in 1892. These "Amazons" were women from Dahomey who fought alongside the male warriors trying to repel the French forces during the conquest of Abomey in 1890. The presence of these armed women warriors grew to mythic status (see Preston-Blier 2002: 136). Given the extraordinary popularity of spectacles including African Amazons, it is quite probable that this association would spring to mind in relation to the contemporary term "amazone" which referred to the woman rider, her (masculine) riding habit, and to her sidesaddle position. This white Amazon was already the focus of sexual desire, as well as of anxieties surrounding social mobility, virilization of women, and animality.[16] In 1893, a spectacular show featuring a hundred Dahomeyans and twenty-five Amazons was presented at the Casino de Paris and at the Lyon Exposition Universelle in 1894. What spectators savored, according to many accounts, was the amount of flesh bared, and this was in strict parallel to the attraction of the *chanteuse épileptique*. I want to draw attention to the way that the fashion for the Epileptic Singer ran parallel to the fashion for the "Black Savage," and to suggest that the former became indebted to the latter.

Studying French popular culture of the period 1877–1910, one becomes more and more aware of a truly obsessional fascination with exoticism, Otherness, and all things African. The reason for this seems straightforward enough: those were the years of France's colonialist expansion. However, when one looks outside of France to its colonialist neighbors, it becomes apparent that only Germany shares the same degree of intense interest. What accounts for France's specificity? To begin with, the French themselves were viewed by their neighbors as exotic and sexually provocative creatures. This perception is not unfounded, given that some observers have suggested that Parisians are more like the stereotypes of Africans than they want to think. The Other is strangely familiar. This had to do with their reputation for licentious behavior, a love and exhibition of decorative attire and objects, and—in the music hall—a penchant for sex, crude humor, and epileptic movement. If France is uniquely obsessed, this is also tied to the importance of fashion in Parisian life—the constant search for, and making of, new fashion trends.

The Nude and the Naked

It is first the nakedness of the black woman's body that jumped out at the reader of late nineteenth-century magazines. There were innumerable drawings of coquettishly naked *white* bodies ensconced in frothy underwear, nipples peeping out from half- or entirely-removed camisoles, but *photographs* always include veils or statue-like poses in skintight body stockings. These drawings were often censored, and the director of the *Courrier Français* magazine was called into court more than once, charged with pornography. White female thighs could be glimpsed in the flesh thanks to the cancan, as well as the occasional breast in the costumes of the Epileptic Singers, and this was sufficient to produce loud cries of indecency and pornography, but that was the limit of nudity. No such strictures were imposed on photographs of African women: French eyes could feast freely on the African woman's nakedness in magazines and in the flesh in the African villages, at the Expositions Universelles and in the music hall (Figure 6).

The difference between the naked and the nude is summed up by Georges Montorgueil. Throughout the night of the 1893 artists' Bal des Quat'z'Arts,[17] the models Manon and Sarah Brown maintained a nude immobile pose. It was a chaste display of "the aesthetic nude" in sharp contrast to La Goulue—herself often called a savage—who wandered through the assembly with her charms clearly visible under a transparent Indian costume. The artists could not have cared less. They admire the

Figure 6
"At Home Attire of a Bambara
Woman from Soudan,"
Fantasio 1 September 1906.
Courtesy Bibliothèque Forney

nude who poses: she was "the nude for sale."[18] The model is admired as
a statue or a painting come to life. However, this is not the case in any
other ball, where the nude inspires "the excitement of lubricity like the
flesh of the slave at the marketplace." Naturally, it is the naked body of
the slave that comes to the writer's mind when seeking a contrast to the
aesthetic nude. The entertainment industry also used the pretext of the
immobile statue to exhibit the nude female body on stage. For despite the
titles of 1890s musical revues like "A Nu les femmes!," "Nue Cocotte,"
and "Paris tout nu," if they were not frozen in statuesque tableaux vivants,
the lovely stars of risqué musical reviews wore a flesh-colored body
stocking, and this included the first striptease, "Le Coucher d'Yvette" in
1894. Suzy Deguez's sensational debut at the Parisiana in 1905 introduced
"La Danse des cheveux" where her hair served to veil her nudity. (Total
nudity on stage did not occur until 1919, in the revue "Paris qui danse"
at the Casino de Paris.) Every café-concert and music-hall had its "nude
revue," and Paris was proud of its "reputation of refined vice"[19] (Figure
7). At the same time, the fear of syphilis translated into a fear of explicit
sexuality on stage. Efforts to suppress nudity and erotic provocation—
viewed as pornography—were more and more insistent, but pornography
in fact flourished thanks to the attention focused by Senator Bérenger on

sex in the theaters and in the music halls. In his December 14 1901 drawing, "Censorship and the nude," Lucien Métivet parodies the efforts to limit nudity. (Figure 8) The caption reads: "to fix once and for all the limits of décolletage on our different stages, the Direction of Beaux-Arts has just had this diagram posted in all dressing rooms of feminine artistes. The *déculottage* of male artists will be recommended later." The various limits allow for momentary appearances of some parts of the body, areas where the form can be perceived under an elastic fabric, sections which are not authorized, and areas that the administration recommends covering with multicolored paste. Some revues, like the "Revue de la Femme" at the Moulin Rouge in 1907 presented "chaste" nudity but, as this excerpt from an article entitled "The Audaciousness of the Nude," demonstrates, by the beginning of the twentieth century the aesthetic nude had stiff competition. The taste for both agitated movement and bared flesh created a demand that music halls needed to meet in order to attract more spectators. And here is where the lascivious gyrations and agitated movement—previously associated with Epileptic Singers and now firmly meshed with African dancers—come into play, accompanied, naturally, by the fantasies surrounding African women.

> In Paris, City of lights, a fashion has taken over: the fashion of the nude. It is at the theater while awaiting worse. At first it was amusing, never before seen, delicate, titillating. . . . After one breast, it was the other, and the simplicity of the gesture . . . didn't shock too much. Then, as the upper floors were undressed, the lower floors were too. . . . and little by little, our artists appeared barely belted from the navel to the hips, *in the fashion of Negresses*. But alas, there were the poor girls with sad-looking tits, with tormented abdomen, painfully contorting themselves. *Not content to adopt noble postures, they were asked to shake themselves, to sing little ditties.* And then another variety of nude was dreamed up, the *nu canaille*, the naughty, shameless nude of the people, she who knows no veil, no poetry, who presents herself like meat on the rack. Even the loincloth of the Negro is discarded. *(On ne connaît même plus le pagne des nègres.)* (My emphasis)[20]

As this article makes clear, the barometer for degrees of undress, nudity, and flagrant lubricity is to be found in the bodily and vestimentary fashions of the African woman. The commercial attraction of obscenity—or at the very least, of sexual provocation—was central to the Epileptic Singers' rise to fame, and it is no less central to the draw of African women in the eyes of the media. Labeled "animalistically aggressive" like Africans, both in dress and in song lyrics, the *chanteuse épileptique* flaunts the assimilation with courtesans, cocottes, and prostitutes: she sings, "The heck with the sidewalks, I work the stage boards. My bed knows no Sundays. Be well advised, for 10 francs anyone can fondle my ass." Eveline

Janney sang "My Little Vicious (Lustful) Circle." (It is easy to agree with
Georges Montorgueil, who wrote that the songs were the crudest possible
confessions of a cocotte.) The singer presents herself as a sex object and
plays up the fantasies surrounding her body. Some had no choice regard-
ing physical intimacy with male spectators: their "directors" obliged them
to drink and dine with admirers in the audience, and many café-concert
singers contracted syphilis between the ages of twenty-five and thirty-five.
This may account for the aggressive and even castrating mockery found
in some of their repertory. Another popular song "See How Chic the
Cocotte Is" links fashion, sex as commodity, and the influence of Africa:

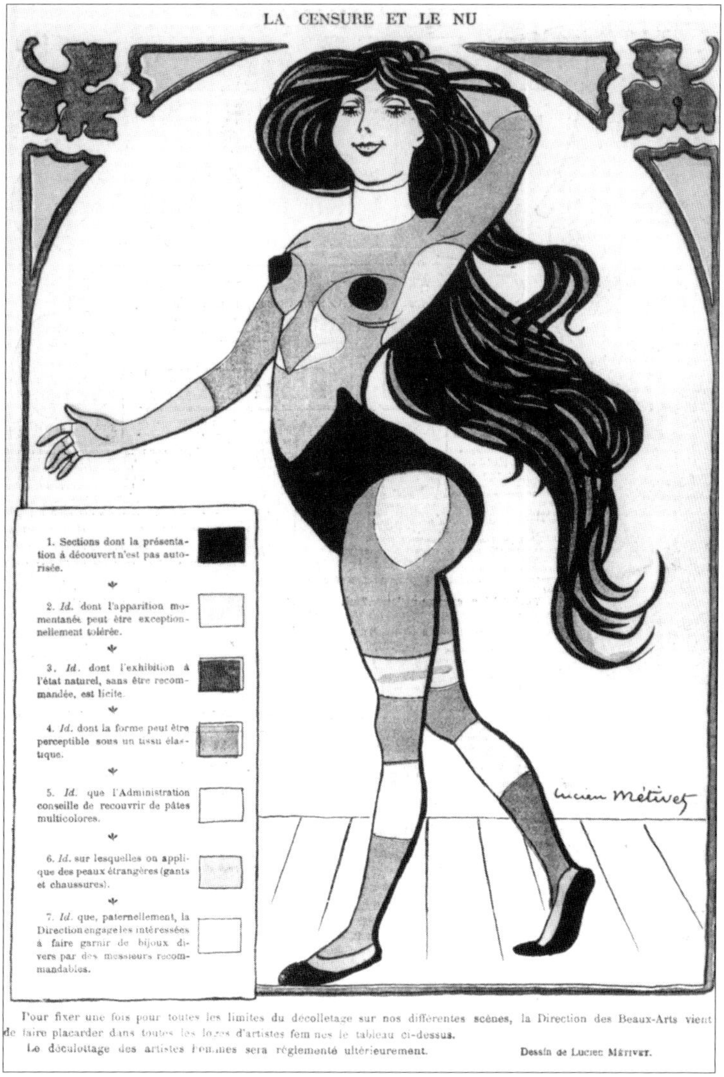

Figure 8
Lucien Metivet, "Censorship and the Nude," *Le Rire* 14 December 1901. Courtesy Bib. Forney.

the cocotte sings, "I'm not a savage, but to please me, you have to cover me with gold." Yet, singers perform in a way that is grotesque or *comical* enough to make the frightening aspects palatable. Later, Josephine Baker would temper the "man-eating" threat of the highly sexualized "black savage" by crossing her eyes.

The body of the Hottentot Venus was by far the most popularized image of a black woman in the nineteenth century, from cartoons to the theater. The primitive sexual appetites of the black woman were supposedly displayed most clearly by her buttocks, which constituted the primary visual attraction when she was exhibited. Scientific theories about sexual deviance were rife in the nineteenth century, and often preposterous. Sartjie Baartman's genitalia, covered by a loincloth, were also the focus of countless fantasies and rumored to be strangely extended like an apron. Post-mortem studies of the genitalia supposedly established links between the sexuality of the black woman, the lesbian and the prostitute, as well as implying freakishness and bestiality. At the end of the nineteenth century, Cesare Lombroso again pointed out the analogy between the physical characteristics of the Hottentot Venus and prostitutes.[21] The prostitute is "an atavistic form of humanity," and her unbridled sexuality is a regression to a primitive stage of evolutionary development, just like the hysteric's (in Gilman 1985: 98). The prostitute, as studied by medical science, was characterized as having thick black hair, a receding forehead, wild eyes, and the facial asymmetry of the insane. Sander Gilman has explored in great depth the ramifications of nineteenth-century medical and biological discourses such as Lombroso's, which he summarizes thus: "The primitive is the black, and the qualities of blackness, or at least of the black female, are those of the prostitute. . . . The late-nineteenth-century perception of the prostitute merged with that of the black" (Gilman 1985: 172). Continual emphasis on the "instinctual behavior of the savage" and the "inherent" lasciviousness of the black woman seemed to justify the assimilation with the prostitute. This proclivity to prostitution is attributed to the hysteric as well: "The links between prostitution, madness, and hysteria were fundamental in contemporary writing on prostitution," according to Alain Corbin (1990: 298). One of these links was the loss of control represented by unleashed sexuality; another was *the "love of dancing" characteristic of degenerates and of savages* (pp. 303 and 305; my emphasis). It is therefore not only via a common analogy with prostitutes, but through the common penchant for dancing that the hysteric is compared to a savage. Let us now look more closely at the variety of dance movements that helped make the Epileptic Singer the embodiment of woman as modern spectacle, a spectacle that consisted of the poses, gestures, and movements of the prostitute, the hysteric, and the savage.

Dangerous Dances

In the same period that black entertainers were thrilling audiences, innumerable cartoons and satirical pieces about these performers and about Africans were regular features in popular magazines. These images constructed in the last quarter of the nineteenth century, built upon in the first decade of the twentieth, are essential to understanding the public for Josephine Baker and *La Revue Nègre* in 1925. They are also the context for the Epileptic Singers. I now want to argue that the paradoxical combination of clownish postures and an aura of danger, as well as the hyper-sexuality attributed to black women, were co-opted by white stars.

The most famous of them was Polaire, the wasp-waisted brunette. Colette's husband Willy described her as "Vivacious, the whole little body jerks and trembles, like a little steam engine. Her arms nervously extended, fists clenched in front of her, the pretty androgynous head flung backwards, she arches that famous waist" (Caradec 1984: 132–3). In her memoirs, *Polaire par elle-même*, Polaire writes "My *instinct* had me make *crazily excited gestures* . . . I sang . . . with my *nostrils flaring*, with my fists clenched, and even with my toes twitching in my shoes . . . I let my *wild mane* go free. . . I sang bent over backward, . . . with nervous, exasperated movements" (Polaire 1933: 83; my emphasis to highlight parallels with depictions of African women). Every part of Polaire's body, from the contractions of her hands to the twitching feet and the *arc de cercle*, conforms to the picture of nineteenth-century hysteria. The media seized upon the image of Polaire as the incarnation of sexual vice, and that contributed to her meteoric rise to stardom. Yet Polaire's image didn't only draw on comparisons with the prostitute and the hysteric. It reached farther down into the French psyche. Observe the "flaring nostrils" and "wild mane" in Polaire's self-portrait, as well as Colette's frequent recourse to animality in the descriptions of her friend: in the space of three pages Polaire is a serpent, a panther, and a gazelle (Colette 1957: 92–95). And "like all . . . sensitive animals, Polaire always seems to be ailing when she is sad. Sadness makes her . . . droop her cheek on her shoulder like those ravishing little monkeys [sold by] dealers in exotic animals" (p. 99). The comparisons leave no doubt: these exotic animals carry with them the image of Africa. Leon Nemo and Jules Gondoin wrote that her face was that of "a delicate and perverse little animal." This animal, moreover, could not be more modern: it "is profiled on the most modern of Parisian horizons."[22] The attraction of Polaire's animality is augmented by her epileptic movements. In her performance at the Ambassadeurs in 1894, she is "*nervous to an excess*, her amorous hips with their crazy twisting, and her legs . . . each is a torpedo sending the foot flying. With her strident voice, she excels in the *fashionable, nervous, neurotic morbidity* . . . [and] moreover, with the troubling air of the unexpected, a bit androgynous . . . All of this instinctive noise, *incessant stamping and trembling* . . . This, henceforth, is the *genre Polaire*" (my emphasis with the exception of "*genre Polaire*").[23] Only eighteen years old at the time, Polaire from that time on takes credit for "inventing" the *genre épileptique*. Jean Lorrain, novelist and critic, left us the most famous description of the star:

> Polaire! the agitating and agitated Polaire . . . in a blouse tight enough to bring on the spasm (of orgasm) . . . the big, voracious mouth . . . that face of a ghoul and of Salome . . . What a coffee grinder and what a belly dance! . . . Polaire hops around, trembles, quivers, dances with her hips, pelvis, and navel, mimes all forms of shocks and shaking, twists, leans over backward in the form of an arc, becomes upright, twists her . . . rolls her eyes up in her head,

meows, is in ecstacy, swoons, and to what music and to what lyrics!
(Lorrain 1936: 279).

Finally, Colette wrote, "I had applauded Polaire in her epilepsy . . . Polaire
sang "The Portrait of the Pussy-cat" tensing up her entire body, quivering
like a stuck wasp, and smiling with a convulsive mouth as if she had just
drunk lime juice" (in Romi 1950: 48).

Even in 1894, it was getting difficult to find something new to keep
spectators coming back for more. "Singers hunt far and wide for an
original gesture, new poses and costume, and they're right to do so
[because the public] is always on the lookout for a curious new silhouette
or a grimace that's never been seen before" (Montorgeuil 1893: 5). Note,
in passing, the importance granted to gesture (at the beginning of the list)
and to the grimace (at the end). By 1902, the public's interest in the
epileptic singers began to wane, but fortunately they hit on a new dance,
with even more "barbaric gesticulations" and movements, and this new
image allowed them to remain at the top for another few years. That dance
was the Cake-Walk.[24]

Introduced in the 1902 review *Les Joyeux Nègres* at the Nouveau-
Cirque the Cake-Walk became the rage: the next years witnessed a veritable explosion of cake-walk-o-mania! What are the implications of raw
energy (such as is found in the Cake-Walk) when it is exhibited in black
bodies? Physical prowess, naturally, and more. But this energy could also
be seen as a form of devolution. "This dance of our fathers, the monkeys
[is composed of] agitation and twisting in the attempt to bite oneself. The
disorder has an order to it; it is all done according to a far-distant ritual"
(Ponchon 1903). It is February 1 1903 and Ponchon's poem in that issue
of the *Courrier Français* is written in response to the news that society
women are forming an anti-Cake-Walk league. The magazine *Le Rire*
warns ironically that the "Cake-Walk obsession has taken over all classes
of society. Let it be known that this Negro dance is all the rage; its vogue
reached its apex with the Bals de l'Opéra and l'Opéra comique. While
there is still time, [attend] the big protest meeting.[25] A month later, it is
clearly too late: the Cake-Walk has taken over in elegant Parisian salons
(Figure 9). Thanks to the two black dancers on the plantation represented
on the inserted medallion, one can see how closely the fashionable couple
on the song sheet for "Cake-Walk de salon" has copied the gesture and
position of the arms and hands in the dance. Even the dress of the two
couples is similar, if considerably more threadbare in the case of the black
dancers. (A difference resides in the addition of hats to accentuate the
image of elegance that the black couple wants to project.) What has
changed is the facial expression: earnestness has replaced jocularity and
gaiety. Nonetheless, despite the restrained demeanor of the dancers in the
fashionable salon, the kicking and strutting of the Cake-Walk still signifies
regression. As the Cake-Walk spreads among Parisians like a contagious
malady, its poses are rendered by important artists such as Jacques Villon

(Figure 10). What is worse is that it is the very symbol of fashion—the Parisienne—who is partially responsible for the contagion. Naturally, the concern is that this dance that blurs class and race boundaries will eventually *destroy* those distinctions. Result: *everyone* will be savages. In an 1899 drawing by Willette, "How the French are Seen Abroad," a French couple dressed as African natives are observed with fear and mistrust by other Europeans. For, underneath their pretense of propriety (the gloves, parasol, umbrella), the primitive instincts revealed by the licentious behavior of the French are clearly visible to their more conservative, "civilized" neighbors (Figure 11). Indeed, at the turn of the century, Paris represents sexual license, the nudity of musical reviews, and the indecent dances of savages such as the cancan.

Figure 10
Jacques Villon, "The Cake-Walk," *Courrier Français* 28 July 1903. Courtesy BnF

The fascination for the rhythms of the black body in dance was very much akin to the fascination for the crazily frenetic rhythms of the Epileptic Singer. The secret self of the hysteric or epileptic was, like the fantasized primitive black self, a face of the Other. Otherness is always *strange*, and the epileptic singer deliberately foregrounded her strangeness, exploiting its spectacular magnetism. Exotic articles of strangeness, the hysteric and the African dancer were awe inspiring, repulsive to some, and sexually exciting despite (or because of) underlying fears and repulsion. The attraction that this image of Woman held for the French can be dated as far back as the beginning of the century with the popularity of Sartjie Baartman, whose movements the naturalist Cuvier described as "brusque and capacious like those of a monkey."[26] Nonetheless, it didn't become a staple of popular entertainment until the end of the 1870s with the Epileptic Singers. Why? The two reasons were: tremendous popular interest in Darwinism *and* in Charcot's hysterics. The fascination with the hysterical body's uncontrollable epileptic contortions coalesced with the fascination for the excess of agitated movement in African dance. In both cases, the attraction is to the "animalistic" and "savage." The Other

Figure 11
Willette, "How the French are Perceived Abroad," *Courrier Français* 10 September 1899. Courtesy BnF

is the secret self of taboos, of hidden desire, but thanks to the nineteenth-century media, the spectacular bodies of the Other are hyper-visible.

The Amazons exhibited in 1890 in Hamburg and St Petersburg "let themselves be touched and caressed by an openly titillated and ever more avid public." Their costumes added to the voluptuousness: a bustier ornamented with shells and a short skirt. The masculine costume consisted of a leopard-skin codpiece and tall, feathered headpieces, evoking for the journalist "the feathered headdresses of Music-Hall dancers" (Preston-Blier 2002: 138). Society women blush as they watch the "Négresse shaking with obscene gesticulations and making the most indecent contortions with her hips" (Chalaye 2002: 301). The description of this African dancer nearly exactly duplicates those written about Polaire.[27] Polaire underlined her originality in the refusal to be comical. Instead, laying emphasis on perversion and animality, Polaire opted for the image of the *femme fatale*. In her memoirs, she noted that her image was the incarnation of Vice. This is perhaps why the press all the more readily ascribed African traits to her persona. The semi-nude or naked presentation of African women in magazines, in zoological gardens, and on music-hall stages ensured that they would be perceived as barbarous, libertine, and venal. "For the well-behaved bourgeoisie, . . . the image of blacks in the Belle-Epoque is associated with the sites of pleasure and perdition where the women are loose and music is contagious" (Chalaye 2002: 301). Not only are the music and dance contagious, but the café-concert atmosphere encourages "the fusion of the races" (Figure 12). Added to popular perception and associations, the link with prostitution propounded by anthropologists, biologists, and psychiatrists that I have alluded to above firmly established the association of the African woman with vice in both popular and intellectual circles.

Virility

In addition to the exciting qualities already mentioned in Polaire's presentation, a certain gender confusion was present: as we have seen, she was called androgynous by the theater critic Jean d'Arc, and Jean Cocteau noted her effect on both men and women. Colette (1957) mentions the "exotic strength" of her legs under a mulatto's white dress (p. 87). Polaire's short hair was a striking and brazen example of her Amazon-like nature. This gender confusion is not unlike the behavior of other epileptic singers who openly advertise their sexuality and dominance over males, displaying traditionally masculine traits of power, boldness, and the ability to choose or reject their mate. The violence and physical prowess of African women, along with their extreme agility, also made them seem virile. In addition, Lombroso's analogy between prostitutes and African women included "an exaggerated frontal angle such as one notes in savages and monkeys . . . indeed [the] whole face is essentially virile" (Lombroso and Ferrero, cited in Callen 1995: 20). Returning to Figure 1 showing a female Parisian and a male African wearing almost identical attire, we can better understand the implication: a woman who adopts African dress and ornament is not only demonstrating civilization's return to savagery, but is also signaling a gender transformation. In dressing like a savage, she takes on virile traits. As we will soon see, Polaire's example suggests that by taking on virile traits, women become threatening and expose themselves to comparisons with savages. Kari Weil (1999) has emphasized the menacing virility in the perceived animality of equestrian stars in the nineteenth-century Paris circus. These women seem joined to their horses, and were assimilated to female Phenomena in the press. The traits of

Figure 12
Lunel, "At L'Eden Café-Concert — The Fusion of the Races," *Courrier Français* 17 January 1889. Courtesy BnF

animality and virility attributed to the American equestrian star Adah Isaacs Mencken laid strong emphasis on her hyper-sexuality, her racial otherness (she was of Jewish and Creole descent), and her androgynous nature.[28] It is not only women in popular spectacle who become more exciting when gender boundaries are blurred: Sarah Bernhardt was the most famous bisexual celebrity of the period. She was the inspiration for Henry James's *The Tragic Muse* as well as for a far less interesting novel written around the same time: Félician Champsaur's 1882 *Dinah Samuel*. "The great tragedienne . . . makes one's head spin, has an extravagant imagination and [projects] . . . dream, sentiment, and a bit of barbarousness" (in Ducrey 1996: 206). One of her lovers, a young poet, comes to the realization that his idol is only made of the flesh of a prostitute . . . this prostitute . . . haunted him" (p. 207). (Interestingly, the narrator adds, "he bore no resemblance to those Negroes who, when their idol fails to do their bidding, break it in pieces" (p. 207).) When he goes to visit, he finds her dressed as a man. Champsaur, one of the most prolific writers on popular spectacle, draws on the same constellation of elements— androgyny, barbarousness, Africans, and prostitution—that concern us here. The excitation of androgyny continues to be prominent in the 1920s. Awestruck before Josephine Baker's dance performances, Pierre de Régnier asked, "Is it a man? . . . is it a woman?" (see Note 27 for the remainder of the citation). The sexual fantasies that surround the *chanteuse épilept-ique*—hyper-sexuality, perversion, and androgyny—are further primitiv-ized by lending her the traits of an African woman, and linking her to animals and atavism. A famous epileptic singer and courtesan, Emilienne d'Alençon, after years of stardom in the café-concert, performed with a trained donkey act and ended life as a concierge. The journalist interview-ing her in 1902 remarked that "You often finish like you began! . . . Atavism is not a meaningless word."[29]

The same gaze that was directed at the Hottentot Venus reemerges when Gabriel Mourey describes a belly dancer in 1890: "she shakes her gener-ous hips . . . and her monstrous behind".[30] It makes one wonder about the underlying fantasies that the *bustle* may have inspired. I am not suggesting that the bustle was deliberately inspired by the form of the exotic woman, simply that it may have inspired fantasies connected with her.[31] The question of influence is nonetheless evoked ironically by a photograph in one of the weekly features on African customs in 1906 in the magazine *Fantasio*. It shows an ingenious technique to elongate the neck, urging the Parisienne to emulate African women: the caption reads, "the Negresse of the Ivory Coast combats the disagreeable sagging of the neck by a most ingenious necklace whose use we recommend to our elegant Parisians" (Figure 13). There is no scarcity of examples of irony, caricature, and gentle mockery of African customs and styles in magazines like *Fantasio* and *Le Rire*; but it is 1906, and African art has become a more explicit influence on feminine fashion in France.

Cake-Walking Epileptic Singers

Mistinguett danced the Cake-Walk in 1903 before bringing her pet monkey on stage three years later. Polaire had beaten her to the punch: Willy wrote that the Cake-Walk "remained a dance of epileptic savages— and like a representation of colic and the illustration of Vomito Négro,[32] until the day that Polaire was kind enough to dance it on the stage of Les Mathurins" (Caradec 1984: 169–70). This assimilation of epilepsy, blackness, savages and disease jumps off the page like the leaps of an epileptic dancer off the stage. The raw energy and abandon of the body

Figure 13
"The Art of Lengthening the Neck," *Fantasio* 15 December 1906. Courtesy BnF

in the Cake-Walk with all its implications of regression, sexual violence, and the domination of the "lower orders" is imported into France from an "uncivilized" place: black America. Willy may have wanted to distinguish Polaire's performance of the Cake-Walk from what was repulsive to him in the "[nauseating] epileptic savagery" of the dance, but in fact Polaire was already associated with the dark continent. Born in Algeria of an Algerian-born Frenchman, she had "dark skin, a physique one wasn't accustomed to meet in Paris" (Polaire 1933: 81). The *Courrier Français* journalist who proclaimed she had created the Genre Polaire, writes in the article cited earlier that she is "a wildcat whose eyes glimmer in the Algerian nights with bizarre and wild reflections: she was born in Algiers—on the border of dull civilizations [and] the deserts of liberty."[33] Polaire may be *"the most Parisienne* among Parisians," according to Nemo and Gondoin, but she is nevertheless more the "daughter of Africa with her languorous eyes brilliant with sunshine, and the slow lascivious walk of women from *down there*, with ardent melancholy, a big night butterfly came to rest on the sky of Paris."[34] Her dark skin and her excessively narrow waist (which accentuated her hips) were the reason that "people insisted on only seeing me as a Phenomenon (*une phénomène*)." In the context of the music hall, as I have noted, the term *Phénomène* has a very precise meaning, akin to "freak." What made Polaire a phenomenon was also her physique, but—as we see from her own description— not only the famous wasp-waist. She mentions her wild mane twice in her memoirs. She cropped her hair short—just above the shoulder—in 1900: twenty years before other "liberated" women all rushed out to "bob" their hair in order to conform to fashion.[35] This and her narrow waist explain her being billed in America as "The Ugliest Woman in the World," a billing that confirms the above equation between Phenomenon and freak. For there was a precedent in America for the billing: it was Julia Pastrana, a bearded Mexican-Indian woman with features called "simian" features and "yellow-brown skin" who sang and danced between 1854 and 1860; Pastrana was also sometimes billed as a freak, "The Apewoman."[36]

In an interview for the magazine *Comoedia Illustrée*, Polaire confessed: "I knew I was more strange than pretty, I felt myself more capable of emotion and passion than of comedy, what was I doing—despite the success and money—on a music-hall stage?"[37] And in a *Fantasio* interview, after describing her childhood in Algeria where she was "surrounded by little Negroes" who admired her belly-dancing, she asks another leading question, but one that we should have no trouble answering: "the little Savage has not only become a Parisienne, but one of the most representative silhouettes of Paris, this Paris that brings all forms of paradox into being. How did that happen?"[38] The answer is obvious: the paradoxical mixture of an aura of the primitive, of hysteria, and of Parisian chic became in fact the key to success: in the 1890s when Polaire became a star, the demand for "savages" on Paris music-hall stages was particularly strong.

Polaire wrote that people found her short hair disgusting, and petulant, she insistently repeated that her "wild mane" was wavy, but not frizzy. When she appeared at Les Ambassadeurs in the early 1890s, already a star, she became fodder for humorists and caricaturists, and this continued into the twentieth century. "Sem, whom all his colleagues soon imitated, represented me with a ring in my nose and the black curls of a *Négresse*. Always the same error about my hair: it was neither black nor curly. . . . Sem ornamented my body with enough rotundities to put the Hottentot Venus to shame!" (Polaire 1933: 93). Photographs of Polaire show her to have dark, wavy hair, but the caricaturist's transformation is easily understood: he is simply completing a picture of sexuality and Phenomenon that includes blackness. Polaire may not have known why people always made the mistake, but the reader has understood: epileptic contortions and fever-pitched sexuality immediately brought associations with blackness. In his 1914 *Album*, Sem goes even further. Polaire surges forth in the midst of the fashionable Parisiennes who look like savages to the artist; she is "the supreme horror . . . a cannibal with frizzy hair . . . her body strangulated, almost cut in half" (Sem 1914: 6–7).[39] Although Sem is traversed with horror by the sight of the fashionable Parisienne—and by Polaire who epitomizes its essence—once again we can observe that the modernity of the fashionable silhouette is assimilated with the image of a savage. One begins to grasp the full measure of the hostility directed at the young performer which, as we see from this example, continued throughout her career. (Sem's first cruel caricatures of her date from around 1900.) Polaire's extraordinary appeal as the incarnation of Vice must also include the "*Négresse's* sexual savagery," and I venture to say that she knew that very well. Now that we've seen the image of the Hottentot Venus spring to Polaire's mind, we can be certain that the term "Phénomène" did not occur innocently in her memoirs. For in fact, the first female Phenomenon to be exhibited in Paris in the nineteenth century was none other than Sartjie Baartman. It was not for nothing that Polaire and another dark-haired Epileptic Singer, Eugénie Fougère, a Spanish Jew, were the first white stars to dance the Cake-Walk in Paris; as with Adah Isaacs Mencken, we again see the conflation of Jewish and Black identity. With the appropriation of the Cake-Walk, the hip-twisting white savage of the café-concert encouraged the oblique aura of racial attributes that already hovered around her to become a more explicit part of her persona.

The fashion for the performance style that I have described here extended to all classes of society in the last quarter of the nineteenth century, and we have seen the preponderant role played by exotic dances from Africa, Spain, and America. Yet, only a generation later, this seems to have been forgotten, as a 1921 interview with Eugénie Fougère makes clear. At the same time as the interviewer credits Fougère as "a precursor who introduced the repertoire of foreign songs and dances from every country into the café-concert," he adds that this was "well before this repertoire became fashionable"[40] This is why, he explains, the singer trying to make a comeback in 1920–1 is "more than ever of her time." Of course, we know that "foreign songs and dances" were a sensational attraction between 1878 and 1900, thanks in very large part to the Paris Expositions Universelles. Cléo de Mérode, for example, famously performed Cambodian dances, and an Epileptic Singer, Lydia, sang "chansons exotiques" at the 1900 Exposition alongside Javanese, Gypsy, Spanish, and Russian dancers. Les Darlings' Girls [sic] presented a tamed-down version of the New Caledonian Pilou-Pilou in 1907 (Figure 14). The desire to claim this fashion as a contemporary phenomenon would resurface with a vengeance

Figure 14
Les Darlings' Girls dance the
Pilou-Pilou, in *Paris qui chante*,
12 May 1907. Collection of
author

in 1925 when *La Revue Nègre* would be promoted as though it had appeared *ex nihilo*. It is hoped that the present study has shown how the white savage, fusing with codes of blackness in the Parisian music hall, created a performance of indeterminate racial identity that would set fashion for some time to come.[41]

Notes

1. In Goncourt, *Journal*, December 3 1866, p. 222 (my emphasis).
2. Toward the end of the nineteenth century, the term *café-concert*, in large part due to the influence of the English music hall, gave way to *music hall*. The smaller café-concerts retained the French appellation. For simplicity's sake, in this article music hall is often used for both.
3. Casque d'Or was the beautiful lover of two Apache gang leaders in turn-of-the-century Paris. Thanks to this notoriety, she became a music-hall singer for a brief period at the Bouffes du Nord, but her lack of musical talent was evident. As Armand Lanoux wrote, "she was no Polaire" (Lanoux 1957: 87). Like the famous cancan dancer la Goulue, at the end of her life she was a wild-animal-tamer on the outskirts of Paris.
4. Interviewed after her American tour in 1909, Polaire said that she received true ovations in America, "a success that even carried over into fashion. People wore Polaire hats, corsets, belts, and hairdos. I was godmother to a complete wardrobe!" (BnF, Département des Arts du spectacle, ICO-Per 21238).
5. One of Charcot's successors, Déjerine, boasted that the Salpêtrière hysterics' ward was as quiet as a monastery. In fact, the epileptiform attack no longer occurred and actors and singers thus no longer found it of interest to visit and to observe gesture.

6. Epileptic performance style is explored in my book, *Why the French Love Jerry Lewis: From Cabaret to Early Cinema* (Gordon 2001a) and in "From Charcot to Charlot" (Gordon 2001b: 27). Polaire's link to representations of Africa was first examined in "Epileptic Singers on the Parisian Stage" (Lloyd and Nelson 2000).

7. In her wonderful essay, "Purebreds and Amazons: Saying Things with Horses in Late 19th-Century France," Kari Weil (1999) has studied the attraction of animality in female equestrian performers in the nineteenth-century circus, and my research has much in common with hers. I return to these similarities later in this article.

8. Polus, "Mistinguett leaves the Concert," *Fantasio* April 15 1907, p. 205.

9. Max Viterbo, "Médallion: Foscolo aux Ambassadeurs," August 19 1908, Microfilm Ro 16026, BnF, Département des Arts du spectacle.

10. We might think of Bakhtin's medieval virago of Carnival, an aspect of the world "accessible only to laughter;" see Linda Frost's "Circassian Beauty and Slave" in Garland Thomson (1996: 298), 298.

11. *Courrier Français* January 10 1892, p. 10.

12. Chorea, a dance-like mania involving chronic agitation of the members, was associated with hystero-epilepsy beginning in 1878, just three years after Emilie Bécat created the genre of the *chanteuse épileptique*.

13. See McCarren (1998).

14. The director of the zoological gardens was the celebrated evolutionist, Geoffroy Saint-Hilaire. The spectacle of Nubians transported from Africa and going about the activities of daily life in the Paris Jardin d'Acclimatation was a huge commercial success. Around thirty such exhibits followed up until 1912, and enjoyed the same success. These are the years of French colonial expansion (1870–1910) during the Third Republic. The 1881 Tierra del Fuego exhibit in Paris drew over 50,000 visitors on a single Sunday (the natives of Tierra del Fuego had the distinction of being designated by Darwin as the lowest form of the human race). Only the very briefest sketch of these exhibits is given here; the reader is referred to the work of Nicolas Bancel, Pascal Blanchard, Laurent Gervereau (*Images et colonies*, Achac/BDICE, 1993) and Nicolas Bancel, Sandrine Lemaire *et al.* (eds) (*Zoos humains: de la Vénus hottentote aux reality shows*, Paris: Editions de la Découverte, 2002).

15. *Fantasio* September 6 1906.

16. See Weil (1999).

17. The Bal des Quat'z'Arts was the annual costume ball given by the students of the Ecole des Beaux-Arts and initiated on April 23 1892. The culmination of the festivities consisted of a riotous and provocative parade from the ball into the streets of Paris.

18. "Les Bals à Paris," *Courrier Français* January 29 1899, p. 8. On the subject of the aesthetic nude, La Goulue is supposed to have said "That's the end of the can can."

19. Hervieux, "Frisson de la chair," *Courrier Français* May 17 1903, p. 7.
20. *Fantasio* February 12 1908, p. 809; my emphasis.
21. Baartman in fact possessed the supergenital membrane of Hottentot women. Interestingly, when Félicien Rops said that the contemporary Parisian woman was *"as foreign as a Hottentot,"* he had just made twenty-four sketches of prostitutes.
22. *La Vie en rose*, October 26 1902, p. 9.
23. Jean d'Arc, "Mlle Polaire aux Ambassadeurs," *Courrier Français* April 22 1894, p. 9.
24. The Cake-Walk originated on ante-bellum Southern plantations as a parody of the Master's dances by the slaves who danced it. The name of the dance comes from the prize given to the best couple of dancers. The original parodic nature of the dance was unknown to French audiences and to the white performers on-stage. It is thus ironic that the Cake-Walk be seen as a display of black, regressive traits, and doubly ironic that the white imitation of a black dance imitating upper-class white dancers should be labeled dangerously contagious. That said, however, the specific *type* of Cake-Walk that was imported into France was not the more graceful walk-around, but the type known in America as the comic or eccentric Cake-Walk. (Documents of both examples can be found in the film archives at the Library of Congress.) Included in black musical reviews beginning in the 1890s in programs containing acrobats, singers, contortionists, and minstrels, it was usually the show-stopper. Jody Blake has also studied the importance of the Cake-Walk in France. The Cake-Walk is the first of the prewar dance phenomena that, as Blake convincingly demonstrates, precede and prepare the advent of primitivism in modern art. Although her focus is on art history, our projects converge in attributing great importance to this facet of popular culture (see her extremely well-researched and important book *Le Tumulte Noir*; Blake 1999).
25. *Le Rire* February 7 1903.
26. Sharpley-Whiting remarks that by describing her characteristics as "reminiscent of monkeys," Cuvier "forever destined blacks to a state of barbarity" (Sharpley-Whiting 1999: 26).
27. This continues to be true in regard to the reviews of Josephine Baker's performances. Nancy Cunard described the "cannibal beauty": "the little savage of the early days with her delirious, grotesque dances" (Cunard 1969: 329). In those early days, Pierre de Régnier asked: "Is it a man? . . . Is it a woman? . . . the voice is high-pitched, she is in a perpetual tremble . . . this dance of rare indecency is the triumph of lubricity" (cited in Lemke 1998: 99). These examples are far from being the only ones that demonstrate an extraordinary similarity between perceptions of the epileptic singers and perceptions of Josephine Baker (whose dancing was labeled epileptic by two journalists

reviewing the première of *La Revue Nègre*), explored in greater detail in my book in progress, *Dancing with Darwin and Vernacular Modernity*, forthcoming from Ashgate Press in 2006.

28. Like Polaire, Mencken was caricatured as an African (and as a centauress, to boot). Yet, when she was temporarily replaced at the Hippodrome by Sarah L'Africaine, a journalist writing in *Le Mousquetaire* objected that "a woman who is beauty itself [could hardly be replaced] by a Negresse who is absolute ugliness everywhere except in Guinea or Senegambia" (in Weil 1999: 15). Kari Weil draws precisely the same conclusion from the material on horsewomen as I do in my research on the café-concert: "racial otherness has itself become a commodity, at least in its feminine form" (p. 16).

29. *La Vie en rose* no. 54 (October 26 1902).

30. *Courrier Français* August 31 1890, p. 2.

31. Without linking it to images of African women, Anthea Callen (1995: 95) also notes "the contemporary obsession with female buttocks . . . privileged in representations of women right across the cultural spectrum . . . through to the fashion for knickers and the bustle." The sources in anthropology and degeneration theory that Callen refers to form the basis for much recent work in the literature and cultural history of the period, including my own research. The limitations of the present study preclude elaborating on these theories in detail.

32. Vomito Négro entered the French language in 1808. Its literal meaning is black vomit, and its medical meaning, yellow fever. Willy is using the former sense of the expression with the stress on Blackness.

33. April 22 1894, p. 9.

34. Nemo and Gondoin, *La Vie en rose* October 26 1902, p. 9; my emphasis.

35. The decadent novelist, Rachilde, who preferred to dress as a man, also cut her hair short around 1900, as Emily Apter (2004) reminds us.

36. For more on Julia Pastrana, see Garland Thomson (1997).

37. June 1 1909, p. 313.

38. *Fantasio* November 15 1909, pp. 272–3.

39. Nancy Troy studies Sem's *Le Vrai et le faux chic* in detail. It was thanks to her paper on this album at the Symposium on fashion and the *femme fatale* held at the Fashion Institute of Technology in January 2003 that I was able to locate Sem's image of Polaire. Embroidering on the phenomenon I have explored here—the fashion for pathology (epilepsy and hysteria) and its relation to Africa—Sem portrays contemporary fashion itself as pathology.

40. "La 'Gommeuse excentrique' Eugénie Fougère," *Comoedia* September 12 1921.

41. Marlene Dietrich's "Hot Voodoo" number—both in and out of the gorilla suit—in the 1932 film *Blonde Venus* is but one example of that.

References

Apter, Emily. 2004. "Weaponizing the *Femme Fatale*: Rachilde's Lethal Amazon, *La Marquise de Sade*." *Fashion Theory* 8(3), 251–266.

Blake, Jody. 1999. *Le Tumulte Noir: Modernist Art and Popular Entertainment in Jazz-Age Paris, 1900–1930*. University Park, PA: Pennsylvania State University Press.

Bourneville, Désiré-Magloire and Paul Regnard. 1878. "La chorée rythmique hystérique." *Iconographie photographique de la Salpêtrière, Vol. 2*. Paris: Delahaye and Lecrosnier.

Callen, Anthea. 1995. *The Spectacular Body: Science, Method and Meaning in the Work of Degas*. New Haven, CT: Yale University Press.

Caradec, François. 1984. *Feu Willy*. Paris: J.-J. Pauvert.

Chadourne, André. 1889. *Le Café-Concert*. Paris: Dentu.

Chalaye, Sylvie. 2002. "Théâtres et cabarets: le 'nègre' spectacle." In Nicolas Bancel, Pascal Blanchard, Gilles Boetsch, Eric Déroo and Sandrine Lemaire (eds) *Zoos humains: de la Vénus hottentote aux reality shows*. Paris: Editions de la Découverte.

Cocteau, Jean. 1935. *Portraits-souvenir, 1900–1914*. Paris: Grasset.

Colette. 1957. *My Apprenticeships and Music-Hall Sidelights*. London: Secker and Warburg.

Corbin, Alain. 1990. *Women for Hire: Prostitution and Sexuality in France After 1850*. Trans. Alan Sheridan. Cambridge, MA, and London: Harvard University Press.

Cunard, Nancy. 1969. *Negro*, p. 369. New York: Negro Universities Press.

Ducrey, Guy. 1996. *Corps et graphies: Poétique de la danse et de la danseuse à la fin du XIXe siècle*. Paris: Champion.

Garland Thomson, Rosemary. 1997. *Extraordinary Bodies: Figuring Physical Disability in American Culture and Literature*. New York: Columbia University Press.

——. (ed.). *Freakery: Cultural Spectacles of the Extraordinary Body*. New York: New York University Press.

Gilman, Sander. 1985. *Difference and Pathology: Stereotypes of Sexuality, Race, and Madness*. Ithaca, NY: Cornell University Press.

Goncourt, Edmond de and Jules de Goncourt. 1957. *Journal: Mémoires de la vie littéraire*. Monaco: Editions de l'Imprimerie Nationale de Monaco.

Gordon, Rae Beth. 2000. "Epileptic Singers on the Parisian Stage." In Rosemary Lloyd and Brian Nelson, *Women Seeking Expression: France 1794–1914*. Monash, Australia: Monash Romance Studies.

——. 2001a. *Why the French Love Jerry Lewis: From Cabaret to Early Cinema*. Stanford, CA: Stanford University Press.

——. 2001b. "From Charcot to Charlot: Unconscious Imitation and Spectatorship in French Cabaret and Early Cinema." *Critical Inquiry* 27: 515–49 (Spring 2001).

Guilbert, Yvette. 1927. *La Chanson de ma vie: mémoires*. Paris: Grasset.

Huysmans, Joris-Karl. 1975. "L'Exposition des Indépendants en 1881." In *L'Art moderne/Certains*. Paris: Union Générale des Editions.

Lanoux, Armand. 1957. "La Vraie Casque d'Or." In Gilbert Guilleminault (ed.) *La Belle Epoque*. Paris: Denoel.

Lemke, Sieglinde. 1998. *Primitive Modernism*, p. 99. Oxford: Oxford University Press.

Lorrain, Jean. 1936. "La Ville empoisonnée." In *Pall-Mall Paris*. Paris: Jean Crès.

McCarren, Felicia. 1998. *Dance Pathologies: Performance, Poetics, Medicine*. Stanford, CA: Stanford University Press.

Mistinguett. 1954. *Toute ma vie*. Paris: Juilliard.

Montorgueil, Georges. 1893. "Le Café-Concert." *L'Echo de Paris* December 9 1893.

Paulus (Paul Habans). 1908. *Les 30 ans de café-concert: Souvenirs recueillis par Octave Pradels*. Paris: Société d'Editions et de publications.

Polaire (pseud. Emilie-Marie Bouchaud). 1933. *Polaire par elle-même*. Paris: Figuière.

Ponchon, Raoul. 1903. "Le Cake-Walk." *Courrier Français* February 1 1903: 2.

Preston-Blier, Suzanne. 2002. "Les Amazones à la rencontre de l'Occident." In *Zoos humains: de la Vénus hottentote aux reality shows*. Paris: Editions de la Découverte.

Renault, Georges and Gustave, Le Rouge. 1899. *Le Quartier Latin*. Paris: Flammarion.

Romi. 1950. *La Petite histoire des café-concerts parisiens*. Paris: Jean Chitry.

Sem (pseud. Georges Goursat). 1914. *Le Vrai et le faux chic*. Paris: Succès.

Sharpley-Whiting, T. Denean. 1999. *Black Venus: Sexualized Savages, Primal Fears, and Primitive Narratives of the French*. Durham, NC: Duke University Press.

Simon, Paul-Max. 1877. *Hygiène de l'esprit au point de vue pratique de la préservation des maladies mentales et nerveuses*. Paris: Baillière.

Steele, Valerie. 2003. "Fashion and the Femme Fatale in Fin-de-Siècle France." Symposium at Fashion Institute of Technology, New York, January 24–5 2003.

Weil, Kari. 1999. "Purebreds and Amazons: Saying things with Horses in Late-Nineteenth-Century France." *Differences: A Journal of Feminist Cultural Studies* 11(1), 1–37.

Archives Cited

Dossiers on performers and café-concerts in the Collection Rondel at the Bibliothèque de l'Arsenal (BnF): Foscolo, Eugénie Fougère, Mistinguett, Polaire.

Fashion Theory, Volume 8, Issue 3, pp. 301–314
Reprints available directly from the Publishers.
Photocopying permitted by licence only.
© 2004 Berg. Printed in the United Kingdom.

L'Allure de Chanel: The Couturière as Literary Character

Lourdes Font

Lourdes Font is a costume and textile historian who teaches in the History of Art department and the School of Graduate Studies at the Fashion Institute of Technology. Her publications include "The Calligrammatic Pattern: An Aspect of Modernism in French Textile Design" (Textile Society of America Proceedings, Spring 1999). She is particularly interested in the subject of fashion in art and literature.

In the history of French literature, Paul Morand (1888–1976) is remembered as the author who best captured the frenetic spirit of the 1920s. Like F. Scott Fitzgerald, he chronicled the lives of rich sophisticates, but with a spare style closer to that of Hemingway. His constant travel, made possible by a parallel career as a diplomat, inspired impressionistic "portraits de villes" like *New York*, published in 1929. In fiction and non-fiction, he showed a sensitive attention to fashion: "Don't journeys always begin with dresses, only to finish with other dresses?", he asked in his first novel, *Lewis et Irène* (Morand 1997: 36)[1]. To publicize the novel's appearance in 1924, Morand's publisher took advantage of the fame of the milliner Lewis and plastered Paris with ads reading: "Are Irène's hats from Lewis? Read the novel by Paul Morand!"[2]

Today the fashion historian is likely to know Paul Morand only in connection with Gabrielle Chanel, the subject of his last book, *L'Allure de Chanel*. When it was published in 1976, five years after the couturière's death, it joined Claude Baillén's memoir, *Chanel Solitaire* (1971) and Edmonde Charles-Roux's biography *L'Irrégulière* (1975) on a shelf which has since grown to more than a dozen volumes. Speaking in her voice, the narrator of *L'Allure de Chanel* recounts the lies and half-truths Chanel told about her early life, fictions which Charles-Roux had investigated and exposed. Nonetheless, the character that emerges in its pages is so vivid that the book has been a key source for subsequent authors and documentary film-makers. It is there that we find Chanel's claim: "I was the first to live the life of this century"[3] and her definition of fashion: "Fashion is not simply a matter of clothes; fashion is in the air, borne upon the wind; one feels it, one breathes it, it is in the sky and on the macadam, it is everywhere, it comes from ideas, manners, events."[4] Morand's Chanel is so persuasively real that it is she who has entered into popular myth. Morand's Chanel is the Chanel we think we know. For this reason alone, it is worthwhile to learn more about him and their relationship.

A Preposterous Dinner Party

Since nothing that concerns Chanel is simple or clear, we cannot be sure when she and Morand first met. It may have been as early as 1917, when thanks to her new friend Misia (Godebska, later Sert) Chanel was first entering the orbit of the Parisian avant-garde (Gidel 2000: 125–6). Misia began integrating her into her circle of friends, dominated by artists, musicians, and writers but also including sophisticated socialites and those like Morand, who had always inhabited both worlds.

Morand was born in Paris, into a bourgeois family with bohemian tastes, a milieu he called "the real Paris."[5] His father Eugène Morand was a playwright known for his collaborations with Sarah Bernhardt. Because his father was an Anglophile, Morand was educated in an English public school, an experience that made him a sports-loving "Englishman at heart" (Guitard-Auviste 1981: 39) and allowed him to pass as an expert on all things British. He prepared for his diplomatic career at the Institut des Sciences Politiques, and during the early years of World War I was posted to London, Rome and Madrid, but by 1917 he was back in Paris. That spring, *Le Mercure de France* published his first short story, "Clarisse" (ibid.: 71–2).[6] He lead an active social life, taking everything and everyone in with a hungry novelist's eye, and recording his impressions in a journal. He first mentions Chanel on May 30, 1917. Jean Cocteau, he reports, "tells of a preposterous dinner party at Cécile Sorel's the day before yesterday. The Berthelots were there, Sert and Misia, Coco Chanel who

Figure 1
Coco Chanel reflected in mirrors. From Käthe v. Porada, *Mode in Paris*. Frankfurt, 1932, p. 109.

is definitely becoming quite a personage" (Morand 1963). Cécile Sorel was a glamorous actress; the Berthelots were Morand's boss at the Ministry of Foreign Affairs, Philippe Berthelot and his wife. The dinner party is "preposterous" because of the mingling of a high-ranking diplomat with the other guests—an artist, his twice-divorced mistress, a literary gadfly like Cocteau, and a couturière. Morand seems amused that the least among them in the eyes of the world is becoming "quite a personage."

He understands that society is changing; he attends similar soirées with his own mistress, the immensely wealthy Princess Hélène Soutzo (Guitard-Auviste 1981: 76–82).

Nearly sixty years later, Cécile Sorel's dinner party is recalled in *L'Allure de Chanel*. In Chanel's version, as told to Morand, she had been escorted by her English lover Arthur "Boy" Capel (Morand 1996: 120–1). If true, the absence of Capel's name from Morand's journal entry is curious, for the two men must have met by 1917, and Cocteau would have known of their acquaintance. Before World War I, Capel was well known in France as a businessman and sportsman; during the War he entered politics as a protégé of Clemenceau and in May, 1917 his book *Reflections on Victory* had just been published in London (Gidel 2000: 122–4). Morand moved in the same circles, and if they had not met in diplomatic receptions in London or Paris they had met on the polo grounds. In any case, two weeks after the party, Morand's journal notes that he dined at Misia's, where he probably heard more about her new friend "Coco." Nor was Misia the only friend they had in common—Cocteau and the dancer Caryathis (Elise Jouhandeau), with whom Chanel studied dance, were others (Guitard-Auviste 1981: 86–7).[8] It is quite probable, therefore, that Morand met the couturière circa 1918–1919.

Têtes-à-têtes in the Rue Cambon

The woman Morand remembered meeting, and described in his preface to *L'Allure de Chanel*, was quiet, shy and vulnerable: "Chanel appeared uncertain, as if she were in doubt about her very life, no longer believing in happiness."[9] This is a credible portrait of her during 1918; in March of that year, the ambitious Boy Capel became engaged to an aristocratic English widow, and soon after that Chanel had to leave the apartment they shared; in October, Capel's marriage took place (Gidel 2000: 133–5). According to one of her biographers, late in 1918 Chanel was seen in the company of the rich Argentinian Eduardo Martínez de Hoz, later a backer of Madeleine Vionnet's couture house, and Paul Morand was visiting the rue Cambon for "nightly têtes-à-têtes" (Madsen 1990: 94). In early 1919, Chanel moved to a suburban country house in order to quietly renew her relationship with Capel, whose wife gave birth to their first child in April (Gidel 2000: 141–2). At the end of September 1919, Chanel's professional address changed from 21 to 31, rue Cambon, where as the sole dressmaker on the premises she had the right to call herself a *couturière* in Paris. Isabelle Fiemeyer states that Capel carried her over the threshold at no. 31 like a bride (Fiemeyer 1999: 60). That November, 1919, Chanel created a wedding dress for her younger sister Antoinette; Boy Capel was one of the witnesses at the wedding (Gidel 2000: 145–6). By the end of the year he was dead, killed in a car accident in the south of France a few days before Christmas. Morand would later write that

Chanel said: "This death was for me a terrible blow. I lost everything when I lost Capel" (Morand 1996: 65).

Certainly Morand came into Chanel's life during some of her most painful experiences, years that ironically coincided with the consolidation of her success and her emergence as a woman whose personal style commanded the attention of the fashionable world. Yet in *L'Allure de Chanel* and in the published version of his journal, Morand deliberately gave the impression that he first met her years later, at an informal New Year's Eve party in the salons at 31, rue Cambon, following an evening at Le Boeuf sur le Toit, the nightclub that had opened in December 1921 (ibid.: 7).

There are two possible reasons why he wouldn't acknowledge that he had known her for years. The first is illustrated by Misia Sert's reaction to the 1947 publication of Morand's *Journal,* in which she figured prominently: "Why," she asked a friend, "does Paul write about me so often? Did I sleep with him? I can't remember."[10] Morand's reputation as a prodigious womanizer was well established by the 1920s (Guitard-Auviste 1981: 150, 152). Discretion might have led him to omit any mention of the "têtes-à-têtes" in the rue Cambon in 1918 or 1919.

The second possible reason is more persuasive. He and Chanel were meeting in the evenings to talk about Boy Capel. As Edmonde Charles-Roux pointed out: "Of all Chanel's friends, Paul Morand was the one who had known Arthur Capel the best and unquestionably the one with whom she most enjoyed talking about this exceptional man. Morand himself had felt the fascination of Boy" (Charles-Roux 1979: 68). Capel was exactly the sort of dashing Englishman Morand identified with and admired. Whether they began before or after Capel's death, his conversations with Chanel cemented their friendship and furnished him with insights for the novel that would launch his literary career in earnest.

A Modern Woman

Edmonde Charles-Roux wrote that "*Lewis et Irène* can, in large measure, be taken as a portrait of the Chanel-Capel liaison" (ibid.: 68).[11] Before evaluating this claim, it should be noted that the novel is a landmark in French literature—the first novel with a heroine who is a self-reliant, successful career woman who enters into a relationship with a man as an equal partner (Guitard-Auviste 1981: 80). The first time Irène appears, on a beach in Sicily, it is clear that she is a modern woman. Lewis is attracted to the beauty of her sun-bronzed body: "She was dressed in a black swimsuit, out of which emerged arms and legs shaded with thin muscles, lean enough and very brown . . . Lewis admired her. She had that beautiful terracotta color of Mediterranean skins, whereas he was still the pale barbarian."[12] Irène is also exceptionally physically fit. She can swim faster than Lewis, literally knocking the breath out of him when they race. Irène drives her own car, speaks four languages and most importantly, is in Sicily alone and on business. Lewis, a sophisticated investment banker, has never met a woman like her.

He tracks her down to London, where she dresses for a business meeting in a very Chanel-ish, sporty sweater and skirt. The narrator describes the slim, neat figure under the clothes: "She walked away, her figure dark and distinct, her hips straight, her transparent stockings stretched over her ankles, her sweater where her breasts barely sprouted, a scarf knotted at her shoulder, flapping in the wind" (Morand 1997: 99). Lewis frankly tells her that he likes "your long waist, your long neck, your narrow arms, your narrow hips . . ."[13] To complete the modern silhouette, he commands her: "Cut your hair." "Never,"[14] she replies. In this respect, Irène is not like Gabrielle Chanel, who had cut her hair back in 1917, as Morand, with his usual attentiveness to fashion news, had reported in his journal at the time (Gidel 2000: 125).

Irène, as Lewis soon discovers, is from a Greek banking family, owners of an investment bank with headquarters in Trieste and branches in London and New York. She had been married to a cousin old enough to be her father, who died bankrupt. She went into business because she is "a modern woman"[15] and remade her fortune. Her background, there-fore, couldn't be more different from Chanel's. The character is in fact based upon Morand's mistress Hélène Soutzo, whom he would marry in 1927 (Guitard-Auviste 1981: 124). A photograph of the couple on their honeymoon in the South of France illustrates the success of the streamlined sportswear championed by Chanel and other designers (Guitard-Auviste 1981, Plate V). But Chanel could not have seen herself in the character of Irène. In Lewis, however, she had to have recognized a devastating portrayal of Boy Capel.

A Flawed Hero

Morand sent Chanel a copy of his novel inscribed: "This Lewis who some-what recalls Boy Capel," (Charles-Roux 1975: 68) but in fact Lewis is almost wholly drawn from Capel, beginning with his physical appearance: "beautiful brown eyes, fast and hard, a strong jaw, thick, very black hair, in disarray, a half-open hunting vest."[16] The description of his apparently nonchalant dress cuts to the heart of a certain variety of English dandyism, which had been such a strong influence on Chanel: "an excess of care drove him to appear carelessly dressed in elegant places, because it pleased him to give an impression of strength and of rudeness; that's why he readily dined in a sports jacket among women in low-cut evening gowns."[17]

Lewis lives his life at top speed. He jumps into his ground-floor apart-ment by the window. He eats while driving his car; he sits on the floor, he almost never sleeps and "like all his contemporaries, he and his nerves were victims of the spirit of speed."[18] He is determinedly modern and scornful of the past. He flies to London from Paris, reading Freud's essays on sexuality, looking down with amusement at ports, roads and train stations, "all that human material of yesterday."[19] He works at home, where the telephone and the typewriter never stop. To Lewis, business, like life, is a game: "It amuses me to work," he says. "Negotiating a loan distracts me more than going sailing, setting up a company more than playing poker, that's all."[20] When he and Irène marry and he takes a year's leave of absence, he reminds her that he has been brought up as a gentleman: "I can very easily live without doing anything; I've received an English upbringing."[21]

What drives Lewis is a need to prove himself superior, to overcome "the misunderstanding of his birth."[22] Morand made Lewis, like Capel, the son of a French mother and an English father, but rumored to be the natural son of a Jewish banker.[23] Although educated at exclusive schools, Lewis is not whole-heartedly accepted by his peers. He learned "very young to understand his situation, to suffer from it, and to take his vengeance."[24] This need to avenge an unjust childhood was also something Chanel and her lover had in common. Morand's hero took his vengeance by beating his friends at sports and at cards, and by stealing their mistresses, as Capel had "stolen" Coco from her previous protector, Étienne Balsan (Gidel 2000: 88–9).

Like an Ancien Régime monarch, Lewis has an official mistress, Elsie Magnac, who resembles a Reutlinger fashion photograph. After meeting Irène, Lewis grows increasingly bored with Mme Magnac. He is irritated by "her pre-War bustline, . . . her Marcel waves, . . . the headbands trimmed with kingfisher feathers that gave her a terrifying and laughable air."[25] He also has a little red book, where he maintains a record of "all the women he's had."[26] These number 413 within about two years[27] and include virgins, married women and divorcées from all classes—from rich American tourists to a *première* at Callot Soeurs—whom he has seduced with a "cinematic speed"[28] that today we might call rape. Lewis has searched for the causes of his sexual compulsions. He has found all sorts of reasons, including that he likes to educate and improve his conquests: "cultivate their minds, . . . form their personalities, introduce them to foreign literature within a few days."[29]

Gabrielle Chanel certainly was educated and improved by Boy Capel. In ten years, he helped her to transform herself from the mistress of a wealthy sportsman to an independent career woman. He was the first to recognize that she was highly intelligent, despite her provincialism and lack of culture. He treated her with respect, gave her books to read and shared his interest in Hinduism and Buddhism. At the apartment he had rented in the avenue Gabriel, they lived in exotic luxury, surrounded by the first of the black lacquered Coromandel screens that would be constant elements of Chanel's décor (Gidel 2000: 90–2).[30] As Chanel would later acknowledge, "he formed me. He knew how to develop in me that which was unique . . . He was for me father, brother, my entire family . . ." (Morand 1996: 38).

But as Morand wrote of Lewis: "We must not forget that Lewis does not have a lot of character. Far from it . . . The idea that a woman might not be made to sacrifice herself (and to *him*), would amaze him."[31] Lewis is vain, immature, and selfish. Irène challenges him to change and, for a while, when they are both working at their respective banks, their relationship is an equal partnership. Morand describes the life of the modern professional couple: "Their different activities, their rushed mornings, their interrupted meals would give greater value to the hours spent together."[32] Irène works alone and is highly organized and competent, able to make mental calculations while getting dressed; she is never late and her desk is always neat, whereas Lewis needs his secretary to function and works surrounded by disorder. He admires his wife, but starts to resent her too. Ultimately, they compete with one another—and she wins. Once the balance of power tips in her favor, their modern marriage collapses.

Lewis et Irène is not at all, as Charles-Roux asserts, a portrait of the Chanel-Capel liaison, which was never legitimized by marriage and never achieved a true balance of power. However, the novel's flawed hero was surely not lost on Chanel. The fashion historian can only wonder what she thought of the novel, and if it prompted the thought that had Boy Capel lived, she might have found in time that she no longer needed him.

To a reader steeped in Chanel lore, *Lewis et Irène* contains a number of interesting resonances. Lewis the milliner did play a part in Chanel's career. Circa 1910, she had hired Lucienne Rabaté, an experienced milliner, away from Lewis to help with her fledgling hat shop (Gidel 2000: 86–7). At one point in the novel Lewis the character spots his car parked on the rue Cambon: "He tried to find a sign for some masseuse or milliner, thinking that Irène must be there: nothing."[33] He waits by the car and when Irène finally appears, he confronts her; she admits that her family's bank has opened a Paris branch. She has secretly violated their mutual leave of absence and returned to work. Lewis realizes that work is necessary for her: "You could never give up working; you'd rather die."[34]

L'Allure de Chanel

In 1946 Gabrielle Chanel had given up working. She was at the Badrutt Palace Hotel in St. Moritz, two years into the exile she had imposed upon herself after the Liberation of Paris,[35] when she happened to meet Morand, who was in similar circumstances. The brilliant double career he had established since World War I, as the most glamorous employee of the French Ministry of Foreign Affairs and the best-travelled of French novelists, had fallen apart during World War II.[36] Like Chanel, Morand was unaccustomed to leisure; his imagination had always been stimulated by constant travel and activity. He was bored and worried about money. The War had depleted his wealthy wife's fortune, the Ministry refused to grant him a pension and no French publisher would touch his work

(Guitard-Auviste 1981: 237–8). The proposition that Chanel now made him—that he help her to write her memoirs—must have offered him distraction and the hope of profit. Chanel too was worried about money. Although she was far from poor, after seven years' retirement she felt insecure and hoped that a memoir published in America would stimulate sales of *Chanel No. 5* (Gidel 2000: 327–8).

Morand set to work by letting Chanel talk, in long speeches "rolling with lava."[37] Did he realize that she was lying to him about her early life? Their collaboration would end in apparent failure. Morand buried his notes of Chanel's monologues in a drawer and forgot about them (Morand 1996: 11). Chanel tried again the following year with Louise de Vilmorin, who "unable to wring a word of truth out of her, was driven to despair" (Charles-Roux 1975: 39), but drafted the first half of a memoir that failed to interest American publishers and would appear only after Chanel's death.[38] In the early 1950s, Chanel worked with the journalist and novelist Michel Déon, and acknowledged that in his 300-page manuscript "there is not a single sentence that is not mine,"[39] but ultimately rejected it. Déon was a close friend of Morand's and visited him in Switzerland (Guitard-Auviste 1981: 246).

In 1963, ten years into Chanel's second career as a couturière, Morand was asked his opinion of her and replied: "Chanel is the greatest character in France . . . the most brilliant, most clever, most unbearable genius there is. Déon, Louise de Vilmorin and I wanted to help her put her memories on paper; nothing pleases her, and she is right. She must forge her own form, but in this case, the right cut of the scissors doesn't come easily."[40] The last phrase was a reference to Chanel's method of working—cutting directly into a luxury fabric, ripping apart an imperfect seam, stripping away a superfluous detail. She would later explain to Claude Baillén: "All you have to do is subtract . . . What you have to do is cut" (Baillén 1974: 57). As Morand realized, Chanel did not possess the same ruthless skill with language. She needed a writer, but could not bring herself to let another hand wield the "scissors." Unlike Louise de Vilmorin or Michel Déon, Morand was Chanel's contemporary and as Edmonde Charles-Roux has pointed out, they had a natural stylistic rapport: "The style and tone of Chanel, her art of living all find their echo in Morand's style, tone and writing. These two lived in harmony with their time, Chanel by dressing it and Morand by describing Europe between the wars, already submerged in a mad wave of jazz . . ." (Charles-Roux 1975: 155).

When Morand's notes finally resurfaced in 1975, the thirty years that had elapsed since their meetings in St. Moritz had revealed the depth of Chanel's impact on twentieth-century women. At her death in 1971, she was recognized as a cultural figure of historic importance, "the exterminating angel of nineteenth-century style" (Morand 1996: 8). Armed with this knowledge and freed from the threat of her interference, Morand was able to cut and reshape his notes into a book that is a tribute to Chanel and to their profound affinity. "It is here that Chanel appears wholly alive," wrote Morand's biographer Ginette Guitard-Auviste, "having dropped her poses, her numerous defenses for a moment broken down; but if her strategems were first undone, Morand put them back together like a master couturier."[41]

L'Allure de Chanel is not a biography. Unlike Charles-Roux, Morand did not burden himself with the task of investigating Chanel's stories. The reader is explicitly warned that the legendary Chanel is speaking: "Reality is sad, and one will always prefer to it that beautiful parasite that is the imagination. Let my legend make its own way, I wish it a good and a long life!"[42] Nor is the book a conventional autobiography or memoir. Morand's voice in the Preface blends seamlessly into Chanel's, but "one can sense that he put his own stamp on the Chanel brand."[43] Morand's Chanel expresses herself in language more eloquent and polished than the couturière could have mustered on her own. For example, she describes her appearance and defines an important element of the Chanel style: "I have kept my hair black like a horse's mane, my eyebrows black like a chimney-sweep's, my skin dark, like the lava of our mountains, my character black, like the heart of a country that has never surrendered" (Morand 1996: 20). At the same time, Morand puts words in Chanel's mouth that she would not willingly have uttered, but that nonetheless ring true, such as: "Messieurs Balsan and Capel felt sorry for me; they thought I was a poor abandoned sparrow; in reality, I was a strong wild beast."[44]

Conclusion

As several authors have pointed out, Boy Capel contributed to making Chanel the supremely sophisticated woman she became. After his death, Chanel would develop an understanding of the arts in the company of the Parisian avant-garde and, alongside Grand Duke Dimitri Pavlovich and the Duke of Westminster, she would refine her concept of luxury. By the late 1930s, Chanel's image was a work of art. But it was Paul Morand who gave a voice to that image, in *L'Allure de Chanel*.

Fashion historians should recognize the importance of literature in general, and of novels in particular, in Chanel's life. "Above all, I have bought books; to read them. Books have been my best friends . . . each book is a treasure. Even the worst book still has something to say to you, something that is true. The stupidest novels are monuments of human experience. I have seen many people who are very intelligent and highly cultured; they have been astonished at what I knew; they would have been even more so if I had told them that I learned about life in novels."[45] Despite her friendships with visual artists such as Salvador Dali and Christian Bérard, Chanel's relationships with writers such as Paul Morand and Reverdy ran deeper and were closer to true collaborations. The books in Chanel's library in her private apartment at the rue Cambon—some given to her by Capel and others dedicated to her by authors she knew intimately—were her precious talismans; they formed protective walls around her, like the Coromandel screens. Finally, we should also recognize that the Chanel we think we know—who is Paul Morand's Chanel—is a work of art because she is a literary character.

Notes

1. "Les voyages ne commencent-ils pas par des robes, pour finir par d'autres robes?" An English edition of the novel translated by Vyvyan Holland, titled *Lewis and Irene*, was published in New York by Boni and Liveright in 1925. The passages quoted in this article have been translated by the author.
2. "Les chapeaux d'Irène sont-ils de chez Lewis? Lisez le roman de Paul Morand!" (quoted in Guitard-Auviste 1981: 142).
3. "... j'ai, la première, vécu de la vie du siècle" (Morand 1996: 172).
4. "... la mode est dans l'air, c'est le vent qui l'apporte, on la pressent, on la respire, elle est au ciel et sur le macadam, elle est partout, elle tient aux idées, aux moeurs, aux événements ..." (Morand 1996: 171–2).
5. Morand probably never knew that his father's family had roots in the Auvergne, like Chanel's, and that a seventeenth-century ancestor, Jean Morand, had been a "marchand forain" like Chanel's grandfather, Henri-Adrien Chanel (Guitard-Auviste 1981: 22–7).
6. This story, with two other "portraits de femme" and a preface by Marcel Proust, would be published as *Tendres Stocks*. In each story a love affair is associated with business transactions and sales at a discount. When the book appeared in 1921, Morand dedicated a copy to Chanel and her then lover, Pierre Reverdy (Charles-Roux 1975: 215).
7. According to Axel Madsen, Morand himself was present at Cécile Sorel's dinner (Madsen 1990: 83).
8. Morand's and Chanel's paths began to converge in the spring of 1917. According to Marcel Haedrich, who knew Chanel during the 1960s, she and Boy Capel had been in the audience at the première of the ballet *Parade* on May 18, 1917, an event that Morand also attended and that many remembered as the start of the postwar era in the arts (Haedrich 1987: 90).
9. "Chanel apparaissait incertaine et comme mettant sa propre vie en doute, ne croyant plus au bonheur ..." (Morand 1996: 8).
10. The friend to whom this remark was made—perhaps Chanel, Misia Sert's closest friend—passed it on to Morand (Guitard-Auviste 1981: 151).
11. Charles-Roux is echoed by Axel Madsen, who characterized *Lewis et Irène* as "a successful novel depicting their story" (Madsen 1990: 70).

12. "Elle était vêtue d'un maillot noir, hors duquel sortaient des bras et des jambes ombrées de muscles maigres, assez secs et très bruns . . . Lewis l'admira. Elle avait cette belle couleur terrecuite des peaux méditerranéennes, alors que lui n'était encore que le barbare aux chairs blêmes" (Morand 1997: 99).
13. "Votre taille longue, votre long cou, vos bras étroits, votre taille étroite . . .' (ibid.: 109).
14. "Coupez-vous les cheveux." "Jamais." (ibid.: 111).
15. ". . . mais comme Irène est en même temps une femme moderne, aidée de ses cousins, elle est entrée dans les affaires, a payé ses dettes et refait sa fortune" (Morand 1997: 82–3).
16. ". . . de beaux yeux bruns, durs et rapides, de la mâchoire, des cheveux massifs très noirs, en désordre, un gilet de chasse entrouvert . . ." (ibid.: 23).
17. ". . . un excès de recherche le poussait à se montrer négligé dans les endroits élégants, parce qu'il ne lui déplaisait pas de donner une impression de force et de mauvaise éducation. C'est ainsi qu'il dînait volontiers en veston parmi des femmes décolletées" (ibid.: 25).
18. ". . . et comme tous ses contemporains, il était, lui et ses nerfs, victimes de l'esprit de vitesse" (ibid.: 38).
19. ". . . tout ce matériel humain d'hier" (ibid.: 87).
20. "Je m'amuse à travailler. Négocier un emprunt me distrait plus que de faire de la voile, dresser un acte de société, plus que de jouer au poker. Voilà tout" (ibid.: 67).
21. ". . . je peux très bien vivre sans rien faire: j'ai reçu une éducation anglaise" (ibid.: 124).
22. ". . . le malentendu de sa naissance" (ibid.: 27).
23. By making Lewis's natural father Belgian, Morand departed only slightly from the rumors concerning Capel's paternity, which centered around one of the French Péreire brothers (Gidel 2000: 84).
24. ". . . très jeune de comprendre sa situation, d'en souffrir, et de s'en venger" (Morand 1997: 28).
25. . . . sa poitrine d'avant-guerre, . . . ses ondulations Marcel, . . . ses diadèmes en plumes de martin-pêcheur, qui lui donnaient l'air terrifiant et risible . . ." (Morand 1997: 72).
26. ". . . toutes les femmes qu'il a eues" (ibid.: 33).
27. The novel's plot begins circa 1920; Lewis has recorded his conquests "depuis l'armistice" in November 1918 (ibid.: 33).
28. "Par nervosité, ennui, Lewis mèna ses aventures avec une rapidité cinématographique" (ibid.: 35).
29. ". . . pour cultiver leur esprit, pour leur faire le caractère, . . . et les mettre pendant quelques jours au courant des littératures étrangères" (ibid.: 35–6).
30. Morand, who traveled to Japan, China, and Southeast Asia in 1925–26, had acquired similar Chinese screens by January of 1927 (Guitard-Auviste 1981: 81).

31. "Il ne faut pas oublier que Lewis n'est pas un grand caractère. Loin de là . . . qu'une femme ne fut pas faite pour se sacrifier (et à lui), le stupéfait . . ." (Morand 1997: 69–70).
32. "Des occupations différentes, leurs levers brusqués, leurs repas interrompus allaient donner plus de prix aux heures passées ensemble" (ibid.: 157).
33. "Il chercha à découvrir l'adresse de quelque masseuse ou modiste, pensant qu'Irène s'y trouvait: rien" (ibid.: 150).
34. "Jamais vous ne renoncerez à travailler; sinon vous mourrez" (ibid.: 153).
35. The most complete and most balanced account of Chanel's life during the Occupation is in Gidel 2000: 292–325.
36. Morand had never let his obligations to the Ministry stand in the way of his literary career, and came close to being fired more than once. He had been posted to London at the start of the War, in charge of a task force waging "economic war," but at the fall of France, instead of offering his services to de Gaulle, he reported to Maréchal Pétain in Vichy. After a stint as Vichy's Ambassador to Romania, his last diplomatic post was in Switzerland, where he would remain after his resignation in 1944 (Guitard-Auviste 1981: 234–6). Morand's poor judgment may have been due to the influence of his wife Hélène, who was "ouvertement germanophile" (ibid.: 221).
37. "Cette voix torrentueuse, roulant de la lave . . ." (Morand 1996: 11).
38. Serialized in *Jours de France* (November/December 1971) and published by Gallimard as *Mémoires de Coco* in 1999.
39. ". . . il n'y a pas une seule phrase qui ne soit de moi . . ." (quoted in Gidel 2000: 339).
40. "Chanel est le plus grand personnage de France . . . la femme la plus brillante, la plus ruante, la plus génialement insupportable qui soit. Déon, Louise de Vilmorin et moi avons voulu l'aider pour jeter ses souvenirs sur le papier; rien ne lui plaît et elle a raison; il faudrait qu'elle forge sa propre forme, mais là, le coup de ciseaux n'est pas donné" (Paul Morand, letter to Ginette Guitard-Auviste, May 1, 1963, quoted in Guitard-Auviste 1981: 306).
41. ". . . c'est ici que Chanel nous apparaît toute vive, ayant quitté la pose . . . , ses nombreuses armes défensives pour un instant démorcelées. Mais ses propos décousus, Morand les a recousus, maître couturier en la matière" (Guitard-Auviste 1981: 307).
42. ". . . la réalité est triste et on lui préférera toujours ce beau parasite qu'est l'imagination. Que ma légende fasse son chemin, je lui souhaite bonne et longue vie!" (Morand 1996: 22).
43. ". . . sur la griffe de Chanel il a apposé sa propre griffe, cela se sent . . ." Guitard-Auviste 1981: 307).
44. "M. B[alsan] et Capel avaient eu pitié de moi; ils me croyaient un pauvre moineau abandonné; en réalité, j'étais un fauve" (Morand 1996: 37).

45. "J'ai acheté surtout des livres: pour les lire. Les livres ont été mes meilleurs amis . . . chaque livre est un trésor. Le plus mauvais livre a toujours quelque chose à vous dire, quelque chose de vrai. Les romans les plus stupides sont des monuments d'expérience humaine. J'ai vu beaucoup de gens très intelligents et de haute culture; ils ont été étonnés de ce que je savais; ils l'eussent été plus encore si je leur avais dit que j'avais appris la vie dans les romans."

References

Baillén, Claude [Claude Delay]. 1974. *Chanel Solitaire*. Trans. Barbara Bray. New York: Quadrangle.

Charles-Roux, Edmonde. 1975. *Chanel: Her Life, her World and the Woman Behind the Legend*. Trans. Nancy Amphoux. New York: Knopf.

——. 1979. *Chanel and her World*. Trans. Daniel Wheeler. New York: Vendome Press.

Fiemeyer, Isabelle. 1999. *Coco Chanel: Un parfum de mystère*. Paris: Payot.

Gidel, Henry. 2000. *Coco Chanel*. Paris: Flammarion.

Guitard-Auviste, Ginette. 1981. *Paul Morand: Légende et Vérités*. Paris: Hachette.

Haedrich, Marcel. 1987. *Coco Chanel*. Paris: Pierre Belfond.

Madsen, Axel. 1990. *Chanel: A Woman of Her Own*. New York: Henry Holt.

Morand, Paul. 1963. *Journal d'un attaché d'ambassade 1916–1917*. 2nd edn. Paris: Gallimard.

——. 1996. *L'Allure de Chanel*. 2nd edn. Paris: Hermann.

——. 1997. *Lewis et Irène*. 2nd edn. Paris: Grasset.

Vilmorin, Louise de. 1999. *Mémoires de Coco*. Paris: Gallimard.

Fashion Theory, Volume 8, Issue 3, pp. 315–328
Reprints available directly from the Publishers.
Photocopying permitted by licence only.
© 2004 Berg. Printed in the United Kingdom.

Femme Fatale: Fashion and Visual Culture in Fin-de-siècle Paris

Valerie Steele

Valerie Steele is director and chief curator of The Museum at the Fashion Institute of Technology, where she organized the exhibition *Femme Fatale*. She is also editor of *Fashion Theory*

The birthplace of modern life and modern art, Paris, "capital of the nineteenth century," was also the capital of modern fashion. There have been a number of museum exhibitions devoted to Paris fashions of the later nineteenth century, most notably Diana Vreeland's *La Belle Epoque*, which opened on December 12, 1982 at the Metropolitan Museum of Art. Visitors to the exhibition heard the sounds of "Ta-ra-ra-boom-tee-ay" and Strauss waltzes, while they gazed at beautiful ballgowns by couturiers such as Worth and Doucet. "The mood was buoyant, ebullient, and delicious," declared Vreeland on the exhibition audiotour. "It was a time devoted to the best of everything. Music was everywhere." According to Vreeland, the Belle Epoque woman was "an elegant and graceful creature," society lady or courtesan, who sought to "overwhelm and silence her rivals" through fashionable "female one-upmanship" (Silverman 1986: 69).

La Belle Epoque was undeniably dazzling, but I always thought that it presented the fashions of that era simplistically and romantically, through a cloud of nostalgia. After becoming chief curator (and later director) of The Museum at the Fashion Institute of Technology, I was able to organize my own exhibition on the subject, which attempted to demonstrate that fashion was an integral part of the social, intellectual, and aesthetic ferment of the fin de siècle. I wanted to create an exhibition that would present a truly interdisciplinary interpretation of women's fashion, drawing on the most advanced scholarship in art history, cultural studies, cultural and intellectual history, gender studies, literary theory, and material culture. The representation of femininity in late nineteenth-century art and literature has been the focus of much recent scholarship, but fashion also represents—and embodies—the metamorphoses of the modern woman during the pivotal decades from 1880 to 1914, when the "long nineteenth century" ended with the outbreak of World War I.

In conceptualizing the exhibition, I was particularly inspired by Debora Silverman's ground-breaking study, *Art Nouveau in Fin-de-Siècle France: Politics, Psychology and Style,* which interpreted the vanguard style in architecture, design and the decorative arts in terms of its political, psychological, and socio-cultural significance, by Emily Apter's *Feminizing the Fetish: Psychoanalysis and Narrative Obsession in Turn-of-the-century France,* which explores the theme of sexual and gender ambiguity in late nineteenth-century literature, including fashion writing, and by Eugen Weber's *France, Fin de Siècle,* which presents the era in all of its fascinating complexity.

The development of *la mode,* both as a commodity and as an art form in its own right, appeared to be closely related to the emergence of aesthetic *modernité.* Indeed, the fashionable Parisienne was herself an icon of modernity and, as such, she evoked powerful emotions. Beautiful and seductive, she also seemed to many dangerous and unnatural. In short, my interpretation of the fashions of the later nineteenth century was closely related to my understanding of the fin-de-siècle discourse on women and femininity. It seemed to me especially important to emphasize the sexual politics of women's fashion in fin-de-siècle culture and society. Much of this article is based on the exhibition didactics (wall text, extended label copy, and brochure text) for the FIT exhibition, *Femme Fatale: Fashion and Visual Culture in Fin-de-Siècle Paris* (October 21, 2002–January 25, 2003).

Although the myth of the *femme fatale* goes back to Eve and Pandora, it achieved new currency at the end of the nineteenth century, when the position of modern women aroused particular anxiety. Behind the image of the femme fatale, the irresistably attractive woman who leads men to destruction, lurked the specter of the fashionable Parisienne. Far from

Figure 1

Poster for the exhibition *Femme Fatale* held at The Museum at the Fashion Institute of Technology. Worth dress from The Museum of the City of New York, photographed by Irving Solero, MFIT. Graphic design by Anne Finkelstein.

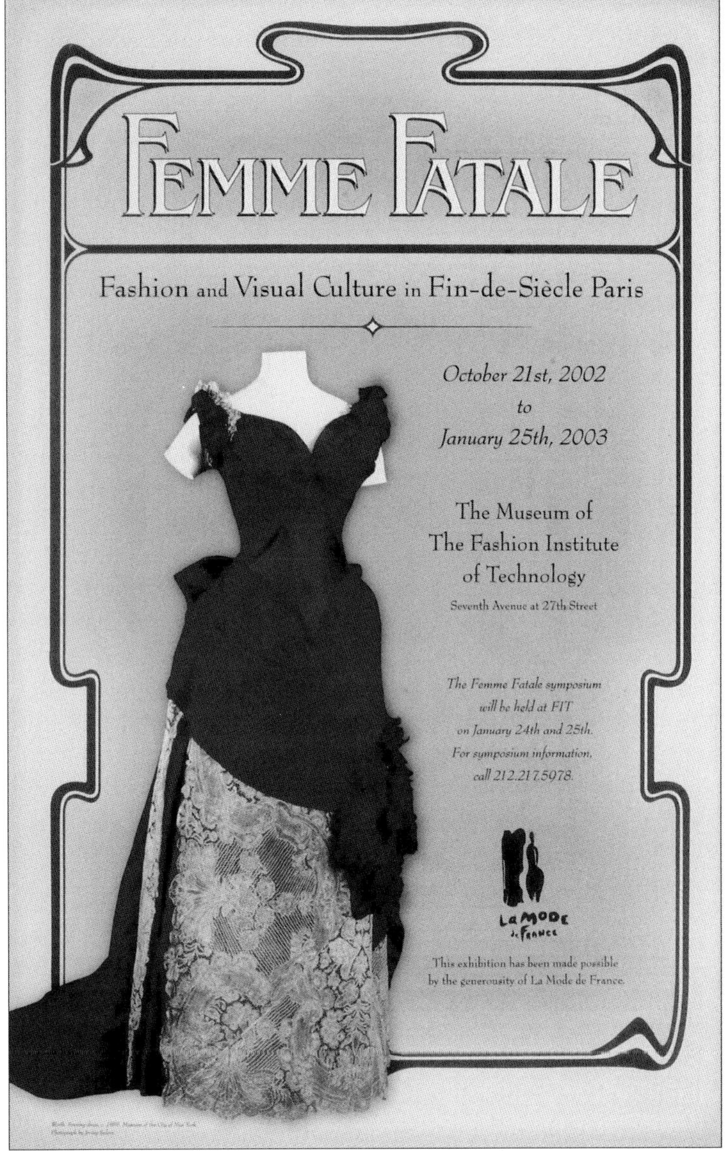

being a frivolous figure, she embodied the metamorphoses of the modern woman and the destructive power of fashion to obliterate distinctions between different types of women.

The first dress that visitors saw when they entered the exhibition was a red satin evening dress by Worth from the 1880s in the collection of The Museum of the City of New York. The silhouette of the dress emphasized the sexually dimorphic curves of the female body, particularly the bosom, the waist-hip differential, and the derrière. The décolleté bodice laced closed in back, resembling a corset. The bodice of the dress was trimmed with crimson feathers and the skirt with ivory lace. It looked like the perfect dress for a Parisian courtesan intent on seduction. Yet it had actually been worn by a New York society lady, which was one of the points that I wished to make.

Fashion blurred the lines between *le monde* (high society) and the *demi-monde*, the shadowy "half-world" where courtesans and actresses reigned. Housewife and harlot alike followed the goddess of fashion. "Clothes, jargon, pursuits, pleasures, cosmetics, everything brings together the *demi-monde* and the *monde entier*; everything allows us to confuse things which should not even be aware of one another's existence," complained *La Gazette de France* (1865). "The nobleman's wife from the Faubourg Saint-Germain passes, on the staircase at Worth's, the elegant female from the Quartier Bréda."

The reference to the couture house of Worth is significant, since fashion itself was in the process of transformation. From a small-scale craft, the couture had developed into a major industry whose products had the prestige and exclusivity of high art. Society ladies and courtesans, French-women and foreigners, went to the same couture houses (such as Worth and Doucet) and they wore essentially the same styles. If anything, the *demi-mondaines* were more likely than respectable women to be extremely fashionable.

Courtesans and actresses in fin-de-siècle Paris were instrumental in launching new and overtly erotic fashions, which were rapidly adopted by respectable women around the world. This was not, of course, an entirely new phenomenon. Earlier in the century, the Goncourt brothers had observed that the courtesan Anna Deslions wore luxurious and expensive dressing gowns and petticoats when seeing clients. However, by the end of the century, such sartorial eroticism had become much more widespread. Respectable women also wore luxurious lingerie and colorful satin corsets. Moreover, French theater women and demi-mondaines, such as the divine Sarah Bernhardt and the beautiful Cléo de Mérode, had moved from notoriety to celebrity, becoming important fashion trend-setters who were photographed and quoted in stylish periodicals such as *Les Modes*.

The definition of "courtisane" in Larousse's *Grand dictionnaire universel* (1867) emphasized the importance of fashion and luxury consumerism: "The *courtisane* knows that she needs a *mise-en-scène* that will bring her close to the man who pays her. In other words, she is a gambler who constantly doubles her stake. She receives one thousand francs per month from an *entreteneur*; by spending those thousand francs on entertainment and clothing expenses, she rarely fails to catch the eye of a spendthrift, who hastens to offer her three or four thousand, assuming that such a woman could not cost any less" (quoted in Bernheimer 1989: 97).

"The courtesan's performance was a matter of surface exhibition," writes the late Charles Bernheimer in his important study, *Figures of Ill*

Repute: Representing Prostitution in Nineteenth-Century France. "She did not signify the sexual body so much as its production as elaborate spectacle. She was artfully constructed according to the codes defining modern desirability. Her appeal was thus largely a function of her ability to dissolve the beastly immediacy of the female animal in a play of intriguing signs and changing masks, all of them lavish and expensive" (ibid.: 96).

Not only the courtesan, but Woman, in general, was fetishized as an art object. According to *L'Art et la Mode* (1890): Woman is a "spangled queen who shines like gold." Fin-de-siècle fashion was characterized by a taste for ornamentation, rich materials and complicated draperies. But it was not merely that women used expensive and elaborate fashions to produce what Baudrillard has called "a production of value through exteriority." Rather, by surrounding herself with all the (artificial) signs of femininity, Woman transformed herself into a new sort of being, half doll, half idol.

At the same time, the vestimentary Old Regime faded into the past, as the ready-to-wear clothing industry increasingly provided the mass market with cheap facsimiles of fashionable styles. Increasingly, working-class and petit bourgeois women followed fashions formerly associated only with ladies of the leisure class. A retail revolution occurred with the rise of the department store, a veritable "dream world" of feminine consumption, where the sexualization of the commodity reached new heights. As Walter Benjamin famously observed: "Fashion prescribes the ritual according to which the fetish commodity demands to be worshipped." The development of a modern consumer culture also resulted in women's growing visibility, and in particular with the phenomenon of "woman as spectacle" in a modern economy of desire.

Foreigners often complained about "the demi-monde fashion mongers of Paris," and claimed to find it shocking that the "daughters of Puritan ancestors" should model themselves on "the fashionable courtisan class in the wicked city of Paris" (Steele 1998). But the legendary chic of the Parisienne was acknowledged (and imitated) around the world. The periodical *La Vie Parisienne* (1889) smugly declared that the fashionable woman "is not always French, but almost always Parisian or she becomes so very quickly. She is sometimes even born a Parisienne on the other side of the ocean." Furthermore, she could be "a princess, a bourgeoise, an actress, or a cocotte."

The stylization and sexualization of women's fashion in the later nineteenth century—like the development more generally of an art characterized by organic, curving forms—occurred within the context of women's growing social and political power. Although the New Woman has traditionally been positioned outside the dominant fashion culture, in reality no such clear demarcation existed. Images of powerful, seductive, and transgressive women circulated throughout fin-de-siècle culture, and were perceived in a variety of ways.

In order to trace the interlocking agendas of the individuals and institutions that produced, promoted, consumed, critiqued, and represented Paris fashion, I utilized a wide range of visual, textual, and material sources. In particular, I drew on the rich and largely neglected body of illustrated books by Octave Uzanne, the bibliophile historian of women's fashion. Just as Silverman emphasizes the legacy of the Goncourt brothers on the creation and perception of Art Nouveau, I sought to demonstrate how the turn-of-the-century discourse on fashion was articulated by writers such as Uzanne, who revived the term *féminie* to describe everything that fell within the domain of women—beauty, ornament, love, and fashion (Uzanne 1896). Like Apter, I proposed a rereading of fashion writing, arguing that it is not, or not just, a genre of egregiously reductive female stereotypes, but rather a discourse providing the possibility for a critical reading of the feminine masquerade.

Octave Uzanne (1852–1931) was a French writer and bibliophile. Editor of several journals, such as *Le Livre*, and founder of bibliophile societies which published illustrated books, he was also a prolific author, who specialized in the art of making a beautiful book. Among his many works are numerous books on women, fashion and society, including *L'Éventail* (The Fan) published in 1882; *L'Ombrelle, le gant, le manchon* (The Sunshade, the Glove and the Muff) published in 1883; *Son Altesse la Femme* (Her Highness Woman) published in 1885; and *La Française du siècle* (The Frenchwoman of the Century) published in 1886. Uzanne later republished similar versions of the last-named book under at least two different titles: *La Femme et la Mode. Métamorphoses de la parisienne, 1792–1892* and *Les Modes à Paris, variations du goût et de l'esthétique de la femme, 1797–1897*. Perhaps his masterpiece was *La Femme à Paris* (translated as The Modern Parisienne*)*, published in 1894 and reprinted in a cheap edition in 1910 as *Parisiennes de ce temps*. He also edited a collection of essays called *Féminies*, and wrote *L'Art et les Artifices de la beauté* (1902).

Today Uzanne is an almost forgotten literary figure, remembered, if at all, as the author of "The End of Books" (1894b), which foresaw how new technologies might result in inventions such as the audiobook. Apter describes him as a kind of "lesser Goncourt," an aesthete, a collector of books and bibelots, and an enthusiast for the eighteenth century. He also produced a rich, albeit still neglected, body of work on fashion, which helped construct a discourse on fashion and femininity in fin-de-siècle France.

It is characteristic of Uzanne's work that fashion and femininity are inextricably linked. Fashion, he insisted, was woman's only "literature," and he himself was the only true "historian" of women's fashion. Indeed, his reputation as a fashion authority was closely associated with his supposed expertise in female psychology. His writings provide a rich source for understanding the significance of women's fashion in the late nineteenth century. I quoted from Uzanne extensively, though hardly exclusively, in the label copy of the exhibition.

Figure 2
Cover illustration by Leon Rudnicki for Octave Uzanne, *La Femme à Paris*. Private collection.

Femme Fatale departed from previous exhibitions on the clothing of the late nineteenth century, because it focused, not simply on the opulence or artistry of the haute couture, but rather on the significance of eroticism in women's fashion. A luxurious tea gown, for example, was presented, not primarily as an example of a particular couturier's work, but as a new type of seductive dishabille. Obviously, labels provided information about materials, makers, and wearers of the particular garments. However, label copy went on to emphasize context, thus facilitating an exploration of the connections between fashion and the image of the modern woman.

The interpretation of past fashions is notoriously fraught with difficulties. At least superficially, nineteenth-century fashion was characterized by a rapid evolution of styles. Yet throughout most of the nineteenth century, the basic form of the dress remained stable, consisting of a fitted bodice and floor-length skirt. We cannot simply assume that changes in style "reflected" changes in women's lives, since there exist internal taste mechanisms that drive changes in fashion even in the absence of social change. Nevertheless, the discourse on women and sexuality certainly had an impact on fashion.

For not only did clothing fashions change, but the discourse on fashion underwent significant alterations, as moralistic strictures against female "vanity" and "immodesty" began to give way to the belief that women should be both "virtuous" and "seductive." This was especially true in Paris, because of the city's historic importance as the "capital of fashion." Fashionable women supported the French economy and French cultural hegemony. In addition to the economic importance of the Paris fashion industries, there were also social and psychological reasons why many men and women developed a greater emotional investment in women's fashion.

Feeling threatened by modernity and, in particular, by the specter of the New Woman, certain men, including Uzanne, conceived of fashion as the art of being feminine. But women also were attracted by this new conception of fashion. In class terms, it enabled nineteenth-century bourgeois women to envision themselves according to an idealized image of the eighteenth-century aristocratic woman as a paragon of seductive artifice. In terms of gender, it implied that, like Madame de Pompadour, they too could obtain power through the exercise of sexual charm. Frivolous as she might seem to us now, the fashionable woman was once considered a dangerous individual who selfishly ignored her familial duties in pursuit of her own pleasures.

"Fashion is women's art, their literature, their science, their history," declared Uzanne. It is women's "religion" for which they would sacrifice every comfort. "They are actresses," he continued, "in love with the effect they produce, anxious to attract attention and to dominate their rivals by the *éclat* of luxury deployed or the refinement of elegance of the *dernier cri* of Parisian creation" (Uzanne 1911: 18, 16). And why was fashion so important to women? According to Uzanne, modern life was characterized by women's growing participation in modern life. There were now female doctors and lawyers, artists and businesswomen. And yet women were still relatively restricted, and working-class women exploited and oppressed (Uzanne 1894).

Adamantly opposed to feminism, Uzanne nevertheless saw himself as the friend of women, and he regarded fashion as a means toward women's self-expression. Modern life had resulted in a growing uniformity, he wrote, both because women were increasingly adopting masculine tailored suits as daywear, and because the democratization of fashion had resulted in mass style, epitomized by the ready-to-wear sold in the great department stores. In reaction to these trends, he believed that women increasingly sought to emphasize individuality of appearance (Uzanne 1911: 9). In *L'Art et l'idée* (1892), one of several magazines that he founded and edited, Uzanne defined taste as "that *je ne sais quoi* that evokes the intimate, the personal, the attractive . . . which is the mark of individual expression."

A refined and individual taste could be manifested in a variety of ways. To begin with, it was absolutely necessary to know the rules governing dress. For instance, sartorial eroticism was closely related to the occasion for which a dress was worn. Nineteenth-century evening dress, for example, was much more physically revealing than day dress, which had not been the case a century previously. As one French writer put it in 1865: "Who among you . . . would dare to appear in the streets and to walk under the eyes of the people in the costume for a ball . . .? The most audacious would not take the liberty . . . for the jeers of the crowd would immediately force her to hide, and the urchins would throw mud and stones at her. Moreover, the police would intervene and probably take her to a safe place, in order to deliver her then to the correctional tribunal, as guilty of an outrage to public morality." Yet the dress that constituted an outrage to public morality when worn on the street was not even remotely risqué when worn at a ball (quoted in Steele 1985: 135).

In his book, *L'Art et les artifices de la beauté* (1902), Uzanne described the contemporary woman, "this new Eve," as enveloped in "a frou-frou of silk and lace." In particular, he extolled the luxury of modern lingerie, those "exquisite petticoats" and "divine chemises" which contrasted so dramatically, both with the modern austerely tailored suit and with the relatively plain undergarments of previous centuries. The modern woman's exterior might be sober and Jansenist, he wrote, but below her dress, there flourished every joyous luxury.

Or as Uzanne memorably put it, "A great coquette is like a flower, . . . who only emits her discreet perfume in the mystery of her intimacies" (Uzanne 1902: 214–15). He was extremely enthusiastic about modern lingerie, which encompassed not only underwear, but all sorts of peignoirs, dressing gowns, and *robes d'intérieur*. "These feminine wraps are of a rare perfection in the most absolute sybaritism," declared Uzanne. "I do not know anything more troubling, more enticing to the eye, more supple, more adorable, more delicate to the touch than all these light, brilliant, superfine veils, of tender and evanescent colors, which are true works of art" (ibid.).

Beautiful lingerie was crucially important, agreed other fashion writers. "It is the veiled, secret part, the desired indiscretion conjured up. The man in love expects silky thrills, caresses of satin, charming rustles." In *La Bréviaire de la femme* (1903), the Comtesse de Tramar insisted that "The husband has the right to see pretty things." Married women should realize that "elegant and gay" lingerie was at least as important as "good silver" or "a well-decorated house" with a "pretty nuptial chamber." In other words, the wife should be not only a homemaker but also a lover.

Intimate apparel became increasingly light and decorative at the turn of the century, in part because of the emerging emphasis on sexual romance within companionate marriage (Steele 1985). This development was not necessarily threatening to men (many of whom, indeed, approved), except inasmuch as women's sexual power might be threatening in conjunction with her (perceived) growing social power.

When Manet's famous painting *Nana* was first displayed in 1877, reviewers argued that any woman wearing a blue satin corset must be a high-priced courtesan: "The aristocracy of vice is recognizable by its lingerie." According to *La Vie Parisienne*, "The proper and virtuous woman wears a white satin corset, never a colored corset." By the turn of the century, however, colorful satin corsets and luxurious, lace-trimmed lingerie had become the height of fashion. The first to adopt luxurious and colorful satin corsets (at a time when respectable women wore modest white corsets), actresses and *demi-mondaines* were also among the first to abandon corsets in favor of fashionable new brassieres, boasting that they did not "need" corsets (Steele 2001).

The *robe d'intérieur* or teagown was a seductive style worn only in the intimacy of the home. Although there were antecedents, such as "the charming déshabillé of the eighteenth century," the new style was really launched in the 1870s with the trend for *le 5 o'clock tea*. At this new social ritual, the hostess wore an elegant teagown to receive her guests. According to *Les Modes* (1901), "The *robe d'intérieur* has become an indispensable element in all elegant wardrobes." This garment was often picturesque or artistic in style, testifying to the wearer's individuality. Because it was usually worn without a corset, it also combined comfort with a somewhat risqué charm. In Proust's great novel, the courtesan Odette is extremely fond of teagowns, which she wears to receive gentlemen friends. One teagown from the 1890s, belonging to The Museum of the City of New York, was featured in the exhibition *Femme Fatale*. Made of Nile green satin, it opened down the front to reveal a pink silk underdress trimmed with fur.

The tailored suit was, for many observers, a sign of the new woman. Because of its masculine associations, it was widely regarded in France as a revolutionary—i.e. feminist—style, and Uzanne was not alone in feeling ambivalent about this modern uniform. According to *Les Modes* (1901), "Gentlemen have not fully appreciated the tailored costume. They have found it too closely resembling their own," making a "pretty woman" look like a "pretty boy." Women, however, seem to have embraced the suit, although they often modified its austerity.

One particularly handsome suit from the Metropolitan Museum of Art was displayed in the exhibition *Femme Fatale*. It was designed by Mme Jeanne Paquin, one of the most successful couturiers of the fin de siècle. (The lyrics of "The Revolutionary March of the Dressmakers" include the verse: "What does the delivery girl demand / Of the House of Worth / Or of Paquin? / More money! / Less work!") With this suit, Mme Paquin skillfully combined the crisp lines of tailoring with suitably feminine color and decoration. The shining curves of taffeta appliqué contrast with the deep-purple velvet ground, creating an effect of light and shadow. The horizontal tucking of the vestee alludes to a man's shirt front, but the effect is enlivened by bright turquoise buttons.

More austerely masculine was a riding habit from the collection of The Museum at FIT. As early as the seventeenth century, aristocratic European women had begun to adopt a specialized costume for horseback riding, which incorporated elements of male attire. By the late nineteenth century, the female riding habit consisted of trousers (worn underneath a long skirt) and a bodice tailored to resemble a man's jacket and shirt front. Boots and a masculine top hat completed the ensemble. Although the riding habit remained traditional, it carried radical implications, because it was so closely based on the prototype of the man's tailored suit. And yet, by virtue of its corseted waist, the riding habit clearly marked its wearer's femininity. Women who rode horseback were often referred to as "Amazons," a term which was also applied to courtesans and women thought to be lesbians. In short, the riding habit was perceived as being prestigious, even "aristocratic," but also highly erotic, and at the same time, transgressive and masculine.

The meaning of any particular style depended on the context and was always subject to negotiation. Black dresses, for example, were standard attire for women of modest budgets, as well as women in mourning. To the extent that black appeared economical, it lost fashionability. "A black gown, no matter how beautiful and well-made, is always less formal than a colorful gown," declared *La Mode de Paris* (1885). "And yet the most distinguished dress, the most becoming, the dress that any woman can wear in any circumstance is certainly a black dress."

The destructiveness of time and the fatality of decline have been part of human thought since antiquity. In the nineteenth century, however, the widespread belief in degeneration emerged as the dark side of science, evolution, and progress. Journalists found "evidence" for the decline of France in alcoholism, drug use, a falling birthrate, and the spread of syphilis. They also deplored the "decadence" of modern art and literature. Conversely, many artists and writers despised the homogenization and mediocrity that they associated with modern bourgeois society.

The image of decadent femininity found in fin-de-siècle art and literature is often dismissed as misogynistic fantasy, associating Woman with the organic/sexual cycle of growth and decay. Certainly, fashion frequently associated woman and nature, many evening dresses being embroidered in Art Nouveau style with plants and flowers. Yet the decadents also focused on artificiality as an escape from nature. Works such as *Les Diaboliques* are filled with mysterious, deviant characters, such as a nervous, dandyish man wearing jeweled earrings and a tall, muscular woman dressed in black satin, "like a human panther."

One of the most beautiful dresses in the exhibition (by the French couturier Pingat) was borrowed from the Museo del Moda y Textil in Santiago, Chile. The New Eve envisioned by certain Decadents might have worn a dress like this, of black cut velvet with a pattern of apples. The iconography of forbidden fruit is here subsumed into an image of the fashionable woman as externalized surface without organic interiority.

Like the dandy, the fashionable woman was, at least potentially, a creature outside nature and beyond gender. Would the wearer of this dress have identified with this "decadent" interpretation? Probably not, but some of those who saw her thus attired may have sensed its relevance.

The rediscovery of the art of the rococo was strongly associated with an idealized image of the eighteenth-century aristocratic woman as a paragon of seductive artifice, as Silverman has demonstrated. The eighteenth century was also one of Uzanne's favorite periods, which he interpreted as a time of erotic dalliance when women changed lovers as easily as they changed dresses. It is significant, therefore, that many late nineteenth-century fashions were directly inspired by eighteenth-century styles. One jacket from the House of Worth, for example, was actually cut from a man's eighteenth-century coat—a type of cross-dressing made easier by the fact that eighteenth-century aristocratic men wore highly decorative clothing.

Another visually compelling dress recalls the fashion for stripes in late eighteenth-century Paris, when the zebra was considered "the most elegantly dressed quadruped." Indeed, it was only in the eighteenth century that stripes acquired positive connotations of chic and youth, since in earlier centuries striped fabric was known as "the devil's cloth," and was relegated to marginal figures such as prostitutes and prisoners. A turn-of-the-century afternoon dress from the House of Worth in the collection of The Museum of the City of New York was clearly intended to recall the styles of the 1780s, and is a good example of the fin-de-siècle enthusiasm for the culture of the *ancien régime.*

The couturier Jacques Doucet was also often inspired by historical modes. One of the founders of the Société de l'Histoire du Costume, he avidly collected eighteenth-century objects, including dresses, and the salon of the Maison Doucet was decorated in the rococo style. Among Doucet's clients were famous actresses and courtesans, such as Réjane, Cléo de Mérode, and Liane de Pougy, as well as members of high society, such as the Vanderbilts and Astors. Again we see how fashion served to obliterate distinctions between respectable women and those of the demimonde.

Many Art Nouveau designs, particularly floral textile designs, recall the sensuous naturalism of eighteenth-century French fashion. Art Nouveau motifs, such as the whiplash curve, appeared frequently in jewelry design and the graphic arts, but less often in fashion design as such. However, one magnificent evening dress from the House of Worth in the collection of the Metropolitan Museum was certainly the *dernier cri* of Parisian creation, and demonstrates how effectively the animated undulating lines of Art Nouveau enhance the curves of the female body.

Luxurious materials, such as silk velvet and sable, reinforced the image of woman as an expensive and desirable object. Exclusivity created degrees of value, as did the style and sensuousness of particular fabrics and furs. A mantle from the House of Worth, for example, was made of a special silk velvet hand-crafted with a pineapple motif, thus alluding to a costly and "exotic" fruit that had to be imported from the colonies. The mantle is trimmed with sable, a thick, dark fur worn by the cruel woman in Sacher Von Masoch's notorious fin-de-siècle novel, *Venus in Furs*. It was also common for dresses to be lavishly decorated with lace, which was regarded as "one of the most charming attributes of feminine dress." As Uzanne wrote, "By its softness and transparency, . . . lace permits the indecision that simultaneously provokes and restrains desire." Lace was also notable as an art form made by women for women.

The *femme nouvelle*, the "New Woman," who left home and family for education and a career, has traditionally been regarded as the antithesis of the fashionable woman. But the reality was more complex. Although the feminist movement in France was small, many women did work (often in the fashion industries) and women increasingly had access to higher education and some legal rights, such as the right to divorce. The respectable bourgeois woman increasingly moved beyond her traditional duties as wife and mother to pursue her own interests and pleasures. New sports such as bicycling made trousers fashionable, while the *amazone*'s riding habit contributed to the development of the woman's tailored suit. Seductive dishabille in the form of the *robe d'intérieur* or teagown entered fashion.

Radical changes were occurring in women's fashion throughout the pivotal decades from 1880 to 1914, when the "long nineteenth century" finally ended with the outbreak of World War I. Moreover, these changes were the result, not primarily of dress reformers' efforts, but of developments *within* the Parisian fashion system. The economic importance of the Paris fashion industries obviously played a major role in pushing fashion forward. But there were also social and cultural forces that contributed to a growing acceptance of fashionable change and sexual display. If men reassured themselves that fashion was the art of being feminine, uniting love and beauty, women increasingly perceived fashion as a means of self-creation and a source of individual pleasure.

Yet the lush ultra-femininity associated with fin-de-siècle fashion and the image of the *femme fatale* became completely *démodé* after World War I. The fashions of 1919 to 1939, associated with the rise of *la femme moderne*, were sensuous in an entirely new way. Corsets were abandoned (or internalized via diet and exercise), and fashion became increasingly light-weight and physically revealing. Of course, the bobbed hair and short skirts of the modern woman also aroused anxiety among many men, as Mary Louise Roberts has demonstrated in her brilliant work on 1920s French culture, *Civilization Without Sexes*. But that is another story, which I pursued in another exhibition, *Fashioning the Modern Woman*, which closed April 10, 2004.

References

Apter, Emily. 1991. *Feminizing the Fetish: Psychoanalysis and Narrative Obsession in Turn-of-the-century France*. Ithaca and London: Cornell University Press.

Bernheimer, Charles. 1989. *Figures of Ill Repute: Representing Prostitution in Nineteenth-century France*. Cambridge MA and London: Harvard University Press.

Roberts, Mary Louise. 1994. *Civilization Without Sexes: Reconstructing Gender in Postwar France, 1917–1927*. Chicago: University of Chicago Press.

Silverman, Debora. 1986. *Selling Culture: Bloomingdale's, Diana Vreeland, and the New Aristocracy of Taste in Reagan's America*. New York: Pantheon.

——. 1989. *Art Nouveau in Fin-de-siècle France: Politics, Psychology, and Style*. Berkeley, Los Angeles, London: University of California Press.

Steele, Valerie. 1985. *Fashion and Eroticism: Ideals of Feminine Beauty from the Victorian Era to the Jazz Age*. New York and Oxford: Oxford University Press.

——. 1998. *Paris Fashion: A Cultural History*. Oxford: Berg, rev. edn.

——. 2001. *The Corset: A Cultural History*. New Haven and London: Yale University Press.

Uzanne, Octave. 1882. *L'Eventail*. Paris.

——. 1883. *L'Ombrelle, le gant, le manchon*. Paris.

——. 1885. *Son Altesse la Femme*. Paris.

——. 1886. *La Française du siècle*. Paris.

——. 1892. *La Femme et la Mode*. Paris.

——. 1894a. *La Femme à Paris*. Paris.

——. 1894b. "The End of Books." *Scribner's Magazine*.

——. 1896. *Féminies*. Paris.

——. 1897. *Les Modes à Paris*. Paris.

——. 1902. *L'Art et les artifices de la beauté*. Paris.

——. 1911. *Sottisier des Moeurs*. Paris.

Weber, Eugen. 1986. *France, Fin de Siècle*. Cambridge MA and London: Harvard University Press.

Fashion Theory, Volume 8, Issue 3, pp. 329–334
Reprints available directly from the Publishers.
Photocopying permitted by licence only.

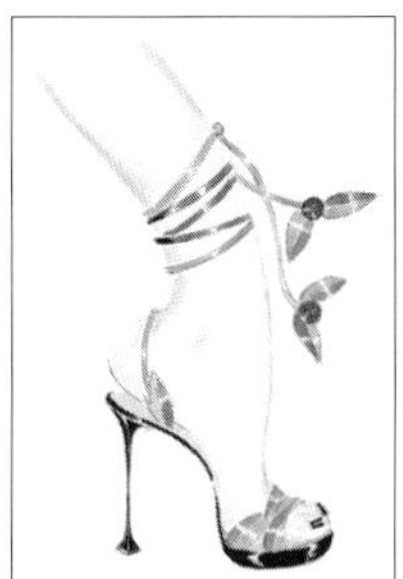

Exhibition Review:
Manolo Blahnik— A Retrospective

**Reviewed by
Janice West**

**The Design Museum, Shad Thames, London,
February 1–May 11 2003**

The design of the exhibition leads the visitor into the labyrinth of Manolo Blahnik's world. Thousands of white shoe boxes pile up to create high walls that guide us through various room settings. The overall effect is that of a visit to a Christmas grotto set in a high-class shoe shop. The first room is apparently a re-creation or at least a re-evocation of the studio where Blahnik designs. His favorite Tombow Japanese brush pens lie on a desk with a pair of gloves he wears in which to draw and the set is strewn with a selection of his sketches. Close by there are cases showing the

Figure 1
Drawing of "Kioto" from
Spring/Summer 2002
Collection, used on cover of
invitation to the press to view
the collection. Not published.
© Manolo Blahnik.

development of a shoe from drawing through clicking, closing, and making accompanied by a display of the lasts that have formed the basis of the shapes that Blahnik has used in recent years. This emphasis on the production of ideas and shoe is the main theme of the show. It is certainly salutary for visitors to see the many components and complexities of shoemaking although some essential elements were missing, for example, the metal shank that supports the arch of every high-heeled shoe.

The wearing of shoes is a secondary concern here, despite the continuous projection of *Sex and the City* across an entire wall in the last section of the show. This is not a criticism, merely an observation that the methodology is clearly design and production not consumption. It is fair to say, however, that without the celebrity wearers there would be no Manolo Blahnik shoes. This retrospective is all to do with imagining shoes and not at all to do with wearing them. This approach is emphasized by the displays of shoes as single items in approximate chronological order, generally lying on one side so that the shoe profile is shown to best effect. Any fashion enthusiast or Manolo fan will not be disappointed by this display. Hundreds of shoes are laid out in this manner and it is fascinating

to see the changes and developments in height, material and decoration, color and shape.

Blahnik was born in the Canary Islands in 1942 and came to London to become a theater designer. At this stage his hero was Oliver Messel and his charming and distinctive drawing style is reminiscent of Messel's designs. Diana Vreeland suggested that Blahnik might become a shoe designer in 1971 after seeing his drawings and the next year he designed his first shoes, for a catwalk show by Ossie Clark in London. At this early stage his ambition outstripped his technical expertise and he did not know how to strengthen a heel. He quickly learnt from his mistakes and there is a later version of his first shoe on display, with two Ossie Clark dresses.

This brings me to the weakest element of the show: the exhibition graphics. Not only is Ossie Clark and Alice Pollock's boutique Quorum called Quorn here (Quorn is a meat substitute) but also the quotes from Blahnik and the hagiographical tone of the text describing his work irritate and amuse the viewer rather than enhance the work. For example the text, unwittingly, I am sure, implies that without Blahnik, Cristobal Balenciaga's contribution to couture would have gone unnoticed.

The kind of breathless prose on display is full of what the late Marghanita Laski (1992) called g-w fashion writing. "G-w indicates a Glamour-word, extremely evocative in the right context and of no real meaning whatsoever." Lest I be thought carping, complaining about words at a shoe show, there is a great deal of text on display, from contextual material to quotes from Blahnik himself. We find out about his encyclopedic knowledge of film, his love of his homes and nature, his adoration for the Empress Elizabeth of Austria (poor Sissy), and how he feels these enthusiasms are reflected in his designs. The tone of the exhibition is thus aspirational as we admire his taste in interior design, gardens, film, music, ceramics, and more.

Of course no designer in any discipline works cut off from the culture that surrounds him or her and it is always interesting to consider the bigger picture but here it does distract our attention from the shoes. The labeling of these is minimal and inconsistent. For example there is a case containing shoes in metal and a flesh-colored latex boot—perhaps these were ones that did not work? Brave of him to show them but irritating that there is no information about them.

There are other shoes on display without captions: a low black mule with red pom-poms has silver sequins inside the shoe where the heel would press down; another is lined with gray rabbit fur. In these shoes the dream elides with the nightmare and the fairy tale changes from *Cinderella* to the *Red Shoes* without comment.

Like Perugia, Ferragamo, and Vivier before him and his contemporaries Jimmy Choo and Christian Louboutin he designs marvelous shoes in many different materials and it is a delight to see so many examples together. But is difficult to see them as anything more than props in a fashion feature when they are so divorced from the wearer.

At first there seems to be a paradox in his assertion that: "I design for confident women who know what they want. I love doers." The last thing one thinks of when one considers fragile silk four-inch heels is doing anything other than posing. But of course this is the key to the fascination of such shoes. They are part of the super-feminine masquerade whereby the wearer stresses the fantasy of her exquisite vulnerability while shod in the acknowledged symbols of success (see, for example, Gamman 2001). No wonder Madonna thinks that Manolo's are better than sex.

References

Gamman, Lorraine. 2001. "Self-fashioning, gender display and sexy girl shoes: what's at stake—female fetishism or narcissism?" In Shari Benstock and Suzanne Ferriss (eds) *Footnotes: On Shoes*, pp. 93–115. New Brunswick, NJ: Rutgers University Press.
Laski, Marghanita. 1992. "Cheap Clothes for Fat Old Women." In *The Penguin Book of Modern British Comic Writing*, pp. 304–5. Harmondsworth: Penguin.

Fashion Theory, Volume 8, Issue 3, pp. 335–338
Reprints available directly from the Publishers.
Photocopying permitted by licence only.
© 2004 Berg. Printed in the United Kingdom.

Exhibition Review: Fashion & Textile Museum, London

**Reviewed by
Amy de la Haye**

Zandra Rhodes is riding the crest of a wave. Her "vintage" printed silk fashions from the 1970s and 1980s are the height of youth chic, orders are flowing in for her new collections and—perhaps against all the odds— she has fulfilled her dream of opening a museum devoted to fashion and textiles from the 1950s to the present day.

The project evolved from her desire to find a venue for her own archive of some 3,000 garments, as well as paper designs and silkscreens spanning her career from the late 1960s onwards. But discussions with various museum curators highlighted, among other things, potential problems concerning storing such a large collection and flexible future access should she require it. Not easily deterred, and already a self-confessed "museum groupy," she decided to found a museum of her own and to include works by other designers too. When it became apparent that state or charity funding for her project would not be forthcoming, Ms Rhodes promptly sold her own newly decorated house in London's Notting Hill Gate and formed the "American Friends of the Fashion & Textile Museum Foundation," whose fundraising activities subsequently generated some US$4m. Additional finance has been put up by Rhodes's boyfriend Salah Hassanein, a former president of the Warner Brothers film studio.

Located in the culturally thriving South Bank area of London, the museum—a converted warehouse—is the first development in Europe to be designed by the Mexican architect Ricardo Legorreta. Revealing both Legorreta's and Rhodes's own love of brilliant color, their shared irreverence, and their utter assurance of their own sense of style, the building's exterior planes of brilliant pink and orange are inviting, yet in complete contrast to the local landscape.

The Fashion & Textile Museum's (FTM's) mission statement declares its intention ". . . to exhibit the immense changes in contemporary fashion and textiles and educate a wide audience in all areas of fashion and textile design." Under the ultimate direction of Rhodes herself, the museum is run by Creative Director Gity Monsef, who has a core team of four full-time staff. It opened on May 8 2003 with the exhibition "My Favorite Dress," which showcased the work of seventy leading international designers, including Yohji Yamamoto, Ralph Lauren, Alexander McQueen, Calvin Klein, and Dolce e Gabbana. To represent her own work, Zandra Rhodes chose a silk chiffon dress from 1973 with a print inspired by her travels to Ayers Rock in Australia. This was an inspired choice of exhibition, guaranteed to appeal to a wide range of visitors and to attract the support of the designers themselves, who were free to choose which dress was shown and write their own statement about it.

The museum is like a breath of fresh air—quite literally, as the open doors draw in a breeze that makes the suspended and rotating perspex mannequin torsos sway gently from side to side. With its black entrance curtains appliquéd with the letters "FTM," its dark interior, and wires that trail from the ceiling, the initial experience is more akin to a visit to the theater, and with this comes an associated buzz of anticipation. Arranged on two floors the exhibition space, totaling around 5,000 sq. ft, is painted black with purple and yellow detailing. On silver disk plinths sit rows of three-dimensional, neon-orange perspex capital letters, barely readable but visually appealing, that form the exhibit labels, and alongside these are sheets of paper bearing the same information. The installation was designed by Thomas Heatherwick, and Kerr Noble created its graphic identity.

The exhibition offers an opportunity to examine close-up (there are no cases), and in the round, a superb variety of modern dresses—most of which, not surprisingly, are for evening wear, as it is in this area that designers can give their imaginations full reign. There is testimony from each designer about how their choice of dress relates to their vision and

Figure 1
Installation shot from "My Favorite Dress." Photo by Patrick Anderson.

output, but otherwise there is no contextual interpretation or analysis. This might have been achieved by thematic or chronological groupings of objects, but part of the appeal of the FTM is its idiosyncrasy, and thus these time-honored techniques of traditional display are perhaps eschewed.

To support the event, UK high-street outlet Topshop has produced an exclusive range of T-shirts with designs by Sophia Kokosalaki, Moschino, Sonia Rykiel, and Zandra Rhodes herself, with all proceeds going directly to FTM funds. It is hoped that the museum shop and forthcoming café will also give a boost to revenue.

One of the things that make this museum so distinctive is its emphasis upon learning through practical experience. Rhodes's own studio is on

Figure 2
Installation shot from "My
Favorite Dress." Photo by
Patrick Anderson.

site, and leading from this is another space that accommodates six students who come on intensive design placements lasting from two to six weeks. There is also an impressive education room, established in conjunction with nearby Newham College of Further Education and other partners as part of an educational trust. Already equipped with thirteen computer workstations, the long-term vision is that visitors will be able to access not only the museum's collection but also the collections of other designers, which Rhodes plans to photograph. The archive will also be available via the Internet. In the meantime Tim Hunter, the museum's Education Officer, and Gity Monsef are actively involved in local outreach programs. (They have just completed "The Children's Magic Mural," which involved working with six local schools over the last two years and which has resulted in a huge printed textile mural celebrating the multicultural heritage and artistry of local children.) Monsef also coordinates the work of several interns who undertake research, display, and archiving, as well as security/information duties which they take on with an enthusiasm that adds to the visitor's experience.

In addition to Zandra Rhodes's own works, the collection already includes works by London designers including Biba, Ossie Clark, Bill Gibb, Jean Muir, and Bellville Sassoon. And, since opening, designers represented in the exhibition have also begun offering to donate their favorite dresses. Lacking a purchase budget, all acquisitions are donations, and the museum takes advice on what to collect from Madeleine Ginsberg, a former curator at the Victoria & Albert Museum. Ms Rhodes's own passion for fashion textile design will undoubtedly determine future exhibitions, and this could in turn help define and focus the museum's collection policy.

Although the FTM conforms to general museum guidelines, it has a liberating freedom and spontaneity that few state-funded museums can hope to enjoy.

Fashion Theory, Volume 8, Issue 3, pp. 339–350
Reprints available directly from the Publishers.
Photocopying permitted by licence only.
© 2004 Berg. Printed in the United Kingdom.

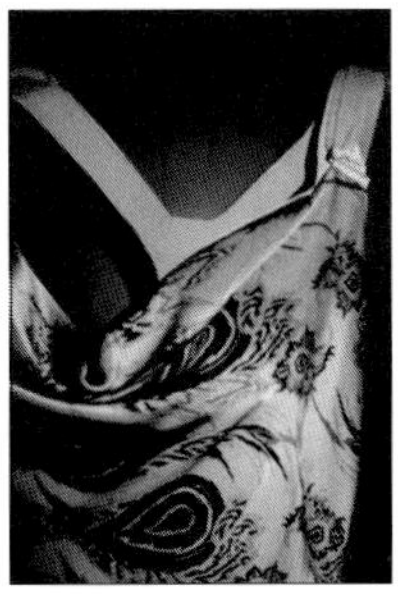

New Gallery Review: "What Happened to all Those Lovely Costumes?"

**Reviewed by
Amy de la Haye and
Rebecca Quinton**

The Fashion & Style Gallery, Brighton Museum & Art Gallery, 2002

After a closure lasting two years, and an investment of around £10m (including a grant of £7.6m from the UK's national Heritage Lottery Fund), Brighton Museum & Art Gallery reopened its doors to the public in May 2002. The museum has been meticulously renovated, and many items from its existing collections re-presented. Conceived holistically, some of its galleries, including Fashion & Style, have become parts of sequences, providing fascinating links between—and juxtapositions of—cross-cultural objects and local history. The new Fashion & Style Gallery begins (or concludes, depending which way the visitor chooses to walk through the museum) a sequence of galleries that addresses issues to do with "The Body," chronicling the diverse ways people represent and transform their bodies, and "Performance," exploring masquerade from around the world.

The first item of costume to enter Brighton Museum's collection was a brown silk umbrella dating from the late eighteenth century and donated in 1897. The collection now ranges from the mid-eighteenth century to the present day, and includes examples of men's, women's, and children's costumes and accessories from Britain, Europe, and North America. Fashion highlights include a boy's silk brocade suit from the 1740s; Nancy Beaton's wedding dress, designed in 1933 by her brother Cecil and made by Idare at the House of Worth, for her marriage to Lord Smiley; and an evening dress designed by Elsa Schiaparelli. On long-term loan is the Messel collection, which gives a fascinating insight into the tastes of five generations from a wealthy and artistic English family. Items include outfits worn by Maud Messel (née Linley-Sambourne), and mid-1930s evening dresses designed by Charles James and worn by Mrs Messel's daughter Anne, Countess of Rosse. The collection also includes the surviving costumes made by Madame Karinska for George Balanchine and Edward James's "*Les Ballets* 1933."

Yet it was not until 1958 that the idea of presenting a permanent display of dress was seriously discussed. Leading dress historian Doris Langley Moore suggested the establishment of a costume gallery, which would combine her own outstanding collection with that of the museum, but while the proposal was greatly supported by the museum it was rejected by the town council who basically did not want it. (She subsequently approached the city fathers of Bath Spa, who offered her a permanent gallery space in the Georgian Assembly Rooms.) It was not until the *Jazz Age* exhibition (1969), in which Martin Battersby presented costumes and accessories in Art Deco style alongside other decorative arts, that fashion was accorded some prominence at Brighton. Even so, yet another nine years passed before dress was allocated a gallery in its own right, and the first fashion event staged in the new space was the *Fortuny* exhibition of 1980, curated by Lou Taylor and originally organized by the Musée Historique des Tissus in Lyon, France. The Friends of the Royal Pavilion and Brighton Museum & Art Gallery had already established a committee to raise funds for a new permanent fashion gallery—holding a series of events, such as a soiree in the House of Lords organized by Lady Elwyn Jones (Polly Binder) which was attended by Norman Hartnell and Laura Ashley, among others. The gallery was officially opened in 1981 by Princess Michael of Kent and was attended by leading model Marie Helvin who stood in front of the case featuring the Adele Rootstein mannequin sculpted to her looks dressed in a Zandra Rhodes ballgown. Curated by Lou Taylor, it presented sections on the function of fashion and an innovative and challenging chronology of fashion from 1810 to 1970.

Exhibits included a punk-rock outfit (possibly the first to be exhibited in a public gallery), a judge's robes, and aesthetic dress from the early twentieth century. A stark contrast was made by juxtaposing a display of 1950s ballgowns by London couturiers Victor Stiebel, Norman Hartnell, John Cavanagh, and Charles James, alongside the street-style duffel-coat outfit worn by a Ban-the-Bomb campaigner in 1958 on that year's CND (Campaign for Nuclear Disarmament) march to Aldermaston.

The fashion gallery closed in 1999 when renovation of the entire museum complex got under way.

The internal curatorial team responsible for the present (renamed) Gallery of Fashion & Style at Brighton consisted of Rebecca Quinton and Angela Charles. Quinton was the museum's permanent Curator of Costume and Textiles, while Charles's temporary curatorial post was funded by the UK Government's Single Regeneration Budget (a scheme assisting local projects emphasizing community and professional training). Amy de la Haye, formerly Curator of Twentieth-Century Fashion at London's Victoria and Albert Museum and currently Senior Research Fellow at the London College of Fashion, was employed on contract, part-time over two years, to work as an external consultant funded by the Heritage Lottery Fund. Her brief was to help develop the Gallery's concept, acquire contemporary fashion exhibits, and revise the museum's collecting strategy. Stylist Sue Milner was also involved from the start of the project, and valuable input came from a team of volunteers, many of them Professor Taylor's design history students from the University of Brighton, who worked on research, preparation and display.

From the outset, it was decided that the strengths and idiosyncrasies of the Gallery's collection should be highlighted and interpreted with a local resonance, while being situated within the broader context of international fashion. This would also form the basis of the museum's collection policy. (It was decided not to take a time-line approach but rather when collecting and displaying 1960s' fashions for example, the museum would target Biba (which had a Brighton branch) in preference to other top designers of the period. When looking at contemporary fashion it would prioritize designers such as Julien MacDonald and Martin Kidman who, like Biba's Barbara Hulanicki, trained at Brighton's College of Art & Design.

Brighton and Hove is a socially and culturally diverse city that attracts significant numbers of tourists. In order for the Fashion & Style Gallery to reflect the dynamics of its visitors, and to engage with them, it sets out to highlight the creative expression of local individuals and the output of local dressmakers and tailors, placing them in the frame together with luxurious and elite international fashion. With this in mind, the exhibits were mounted around four interrelated themes: "George IV," "Renegade," "Internationalism," and "The Collection."

When George IV chose Brighton as a retreat from London in the 1770s his presence did much to transform a small fishing village into a lively

Figure 1
"George IV" case. (L to R) Herbwoman's Attendant's dress and Canopy Bearer's outfit, both worn at the coronation of George IV in 1821; light green wool breeches worn by George IV, 1827 (the waist measures 133 cm). Photograph by Amy de la Haye.

and fashionable seaside resort. He commissioned the building of the Royal Pavilion (a remarkable fantasy palace conceived in a style drawn from both Indian and Chinese influences), where he entertained an international court. He was infamous for his extravagance, and ran up substantial tailors' bills. Few of his clothes survive, and most of those that do are utilitarian items. They include a pair of oversize pale green wool breeches —with a waist size of 133 cm—dated 1827 and made by John Meyer of London's Conduit Street (Meyer also dressed the dandy "Beau" Brummell), and these are on display in the Gallery. A replica pair, made in calico, hangs nearby for children to try on. This part of the exhibition includes dress from George IV's Coronation in 1821, worn by a Herbwoman's attendant and a canopy bearer. These are displayed alongside a fine chintz banyan from around 1780, said to have been worn by the young Prince, which links with a 1760s Chinese silk banyan imported by the East India Company and displayed opposite, in the section titled "Internationalism."

"Internationalism" takes its lead from the Eastern styles used in the architecture and interior decoration of the Royal Pavilion. It encompasses eighteenth-century orientalism, early-twentieth-century exoticism, and twenty-first-century "ethnic" minimalism, together with objects from or inspired by countries along the Silk Route—Turkey, Persia/Iran, India, China, and Japan. When European fashion takes inspiration from other world cultures, that inspiration usually arrives first by way of informal dress and accessories. This section case-studies Indian shawls and the European imitations they engendered, analyzing the development of the Buta motif into the Paisley pattern. More contemporary exhibits include an evening dress from Zandra Rhodes's "China" collection of 1979, and a sheath dress by Alexander McQueen in pale-pink silk printed with paisley motifs (from Spring/Summer 2001). The work of contemporary designers such as Asha Sarabhai and Shirin Guild, both of whom consistently draw influences from their own cultural clothing traditions—Indian and Iranian respectively—presents another facet of this trend. They have each provided an inspirational traditional garment from their own culture which is displayed alongside their own designs.

The "Renegade" section, coordinated by Angela Charles, focuses upon those subcultures that have had a dominant influence in Brighton since the 1950s. Head-to-toe outfits were acquired from the wearers who were seeking personal expression while aligning themselves with one or other of these defined groups. Exhibits include Rockin' Bill's Teddy-boy drape jacket, bootlace tie, and "brothel-creeper" shoes, worn between 1965 and 1969; David Cooke's bespoke Mod suit in two-tone Tonik cloth, from 1965; Tony Lord's 1977 punk-rocker outfit bought at "Seditionaries;" and a "Queer-Fetish-Techno-Punk" ensemble worn by Jed Phoenix between 1998 and 2000. The labels for this section are in the form of testimony from the wearer, accompanied wherever possible with snapshots of them wearing the outfits, or similar clothes. When local school children were invited to respond to the displays before the gallery opened, this was the section that most captured their imagination, and their drawings and comments also feature on some of the extended labels.

One large case is entitled "The Collection" and presents an eclectic array of clothes and accessories, which highlight the richness and diversity of the museum's holdings. It also addresses the perennial fascination visitors have with how and why objects are obtained. Early exhibits include red leather shoes, circa 1820, worn by Anne Jewitt who was the fortune-teller on Brighton pier, and an early 1880s bustle dress made by a local dressmaker which is exhibited opposite another locally made garment, a Neo-Victorian-style Goth outfit (also with a bustle) in the "Renegade" section, made by Sarn V, using meticulously crafted patterns from the 1880s as her template. Items from the last hundred years include swimwear reflecting Brighton's role as a seaside resort, and an evening

Figure 2
Detail of Alexander McQueen printed silk dress from Spring/ Summer 2001. The "invisible" mannequin was sculpted to follow the cut of the dress. Photograph by Amy de la Haye.

dress from 2002 by London couturier Catherine Walker, which updates the museum's collection of English couture evening dresses. An informal, loose, stretch jersey outfit made for a four-year-old child and purchased from a fashionable local childrenswear store is placed alongside the 1740s suit of silk brocade which was tailored for a boy of about the same age.

To encourage interaction between the Gallery and its visitors, "The Collection" space appeals for and exhibits special objects. (For example, when the Gallery first opened, requests for British World War Two "Utility" clothing were immediately rewarded.) The section will also be used for temporary exhibitions each year: the first (curated by Angela

Figure 3
View from the "catwalk" showing the "Internationalism" case, which includes designs by Asha Sarabhai and Shirin Guild and the Indian and Iranian clothes that have (respectively) inspired them. Photograph by Amy de la Haye.

Charles) was devoted to the work of Ben Sherman, a shirtmaker whose company was founded in Brighton and was renowned for dressing mod and Skinhead subcultures, and which celebrated its fortieth anniversary in 2003. Exhibits were drawn from the museum's collection, the Ben Sherman company archive, and lent by local private individuals. In Fall 2005 the museum plans to empty all of the cases to make space for a temporary exhibition of the Messel collection.

The gallery's themes encourage links with other collections and galleries in the Museum. "George IV," for example, is clearly connected with the Royal Pavilion and local history, while "Internationalism" links with the

 Exhibition Review

Figure 4

Black and dark red shot silk bustle dress made by local dressmaker Madame Hawkes, 1880, displayed in "The Collection" case is placed opposite a neo-Victorian-style Goth outfit made and worn by Sarn V, 2001, in "Renegade". Photograph by Amy de la Haye.

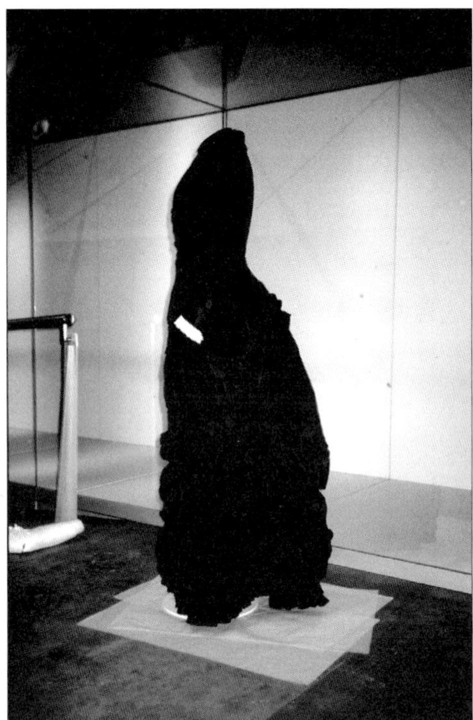

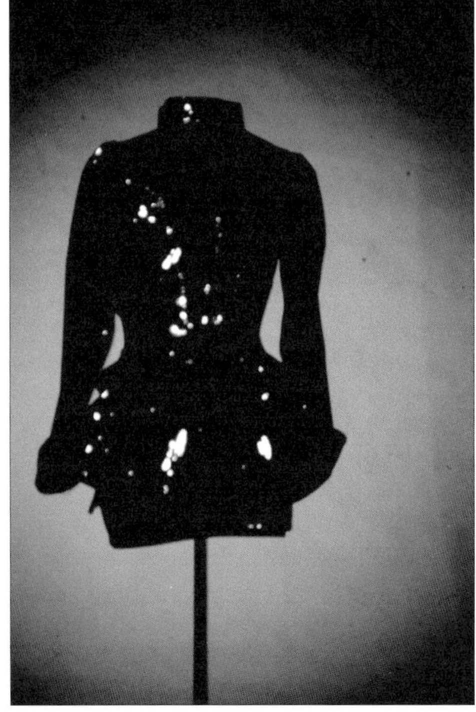

World Art Collection and Oriental-style decorative arts. Within "The Body" gallery's presentation of ideals of beauty is a fashion theme that includes foundation "stays" from the 1780s, a complete set of mid-Victorian underwear, a structured "Lumps and Bumps" vest by designer Georgina Godley (who trained at Brighton College of Art) for Winter 1985, and a men's fashion corset designed by Mr. Pearl who always wears a corset himself.

The aesthetics and the "feel" of the Gallery, which originally housed the museum's 1890s' zoology collection, and which still features carvings of animal heads as the corbels for the hammerbeam roof, was also altered dramatically. Reacting to criticisms that the previous fashion gallery, with its mahogany cases built from the original cases and low light levels felt "dark and spooky," the designers were briefed to conceive a space with four "floating" glass cases, which would permit objects to be viewed from every angle. By enabling visitors to see through the cases, this also avoids concealed spaces and dark corners. The traditional casing and plinth design of galleries and costume exhibitions usually involves elevated displays. These serve to place the clothes—usually luxury fashions—on a pedestal, as well as visually elongating their appearance. As many of the clothes to be displayed in Brighton's Fashion & Style Gallery were made or worn by local residents, and not intended to promote fashion ideals for slender, elongated lines, the garments are presented at visitor level, permitting close-up scrutiny of the objects as well as facilitating a realistic perspective. As the museum is a protected building, sinking cases into the floor was not an option, so consequently a "catwalk" has been constructed to raise the visitor to the same level as the exhibits within their cases. (This also provides an additional and serendipitous element of interactivity, as visitors occupying the various seats around the Gallery begin to look at their fellow visitors' outfits as they appear on the catwalk.)

One of the most noticeable changes from the old gallery is the style of mannequins used to display the garments. The previous gallery employed full-scale, naturalistic mannequins complete with make-up and authentic-ally coifed wigs which were typical of professional curatorial approaches in the late 1970s but which today are less acceptable. Instead an "invisible" mannequin approach was taken—with no heads, no hands, no feet, and with the neckline cut to mirror the line of the outfit displayed. This overcame the problem of creating a unified look while accommodating the differing requirements of displaying clothing worn by an eighteenth-century child, a Prince, a Punk and a contemporary high-fashion outfit. The mannequins were necessarily height adjustable and also avoided the complexity and cost of wigs and cosmetics. Outfits that came with hats are displayed on mannequins with skull-cap-shaped supports and foot-wear is displayed at the base.

The mannequins themselves were standard papier-mâché bust forms, which were customized by the Redevelopment Project's 3-D Design Technician, Jessica Elliott. Necklines were cut to the correct décolletage,

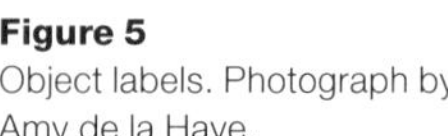

Figure 5
Object labels. Photograph by
Amy de la Haye.

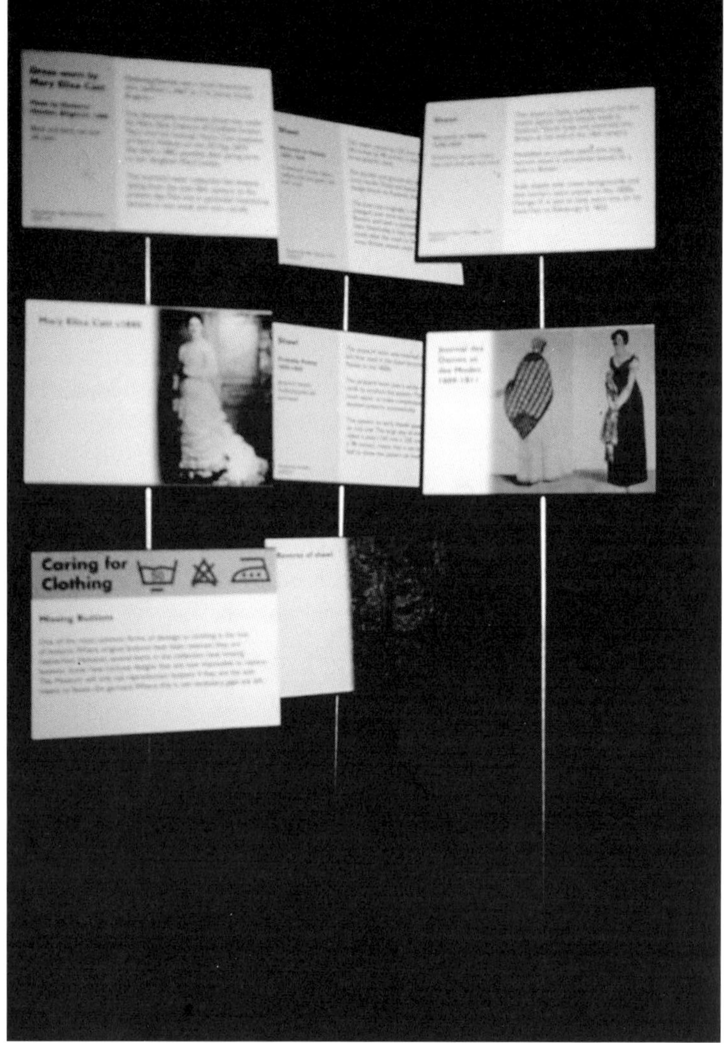

busts reduced, waistlines slimmed and the whole painted to match the
main color of the outfit. Those garments which called for larger, or more
hour-glass-shaped mounts were padded out and adjusted to fit toiles of
the items. These, together with underpinnings and arms, were made by
the Gallery team with the assistance of volunteers from the University of
Brighton: Jan Fielding, Jane Hattrick, June Neville, Mary Allison, Pauline
Heatherington, and Aimée Payton. Mannequin bases were designed with
slender aluminum poles, offset for outfits with bifurcated garments, and
the flat circular bases were powder-coated to match the base of the cases.
All these elements added to the "light and airy" look of the Gallery, with
the outfits seeming to hover above the ground.

The Gallery itself has been designed to offer a range of different levels of interpretation. A short introductory text panel is displayed next to each entrance to the Gallery, with a further text panel inside each exhibition case. Each mannequin has its accompanying main label, with object-specific details on the left and a couple of paragraphs of contextual information on the right. As a local- authority-run museum, one of its primary audiences is school children, so labels were limited to a hundred words each, and a reading age assumed of approximately twelve. Specialist terms, such as brocade or banyan, have been used, but followed by a brief description in brackets. Many exhibits have supplementary information on second, and sometimes third, labels, mounted below the main panel. These might include images of the original wearer, the comments and drawings by school children on the "Renegade" outfits, and an explanation of some of the Gallery's conservation issues, such as the low light levels or to what extent items have been conserved with regard to tears, stains, and missing buttons.

The two outfits from George IV's Coronation have a supporting video showing preliminary watercolor sketches and the finished engravings from one of the major commemorative books. Setting the costumes in the context of the coronation procession, these show the extent of the extravagance involved, a curious fusion of Jacobean and neoclassical styling. A multimedia program, designed by Cognitive Applications, enhances the "Renegade" case. By the use of a simple touch-screen the visitor can access over seventy-five oral histories, approximately five hundred images, and various music and video snippets that look at the clothing within a wider context of its subculture.

Alongside one of the multimedia kiosks is a study area with a small and changing selection of relevant book and magazines. Extended information booklets on each of the four themes are planned for future publication, and will be available in this area. Another interactive component is a set of calico toiles of garments on display or in the remainder of the collection. Full reproductions had been planned; however, the cost of these, together with the difficulty of sourcing suitable materials for the older pieces, and their subsequent care—especially in an unsupervised activity—would have been prohibitive. Instead, an ongoing project was set up by volunteer Jan Fielding to make toiles from patterns of the original garments. This has resulted in a popular activity for both children and adults, especially the copy of George IV's voluminous breeches (taken from Remus Au's pattern), and has also added invaluable information to the collection's object history files about cut and construction.

The Gallery has enjoyed favorable press coverage, and visitor attendances to costume-related activities in the first year of opening have exceeded expectation. The Gallery is supported by a program of school and adult educational activities, the latter including lunchtime "Meet the Curator" tours, evening lectures, and handling sessions in which items from the costume collection have been on open supervised view to visitors.

Public demand has led to the first print-run of selected postcards of exhibits in the gallery.

Phase II of the redevelopment of Brighton Museum & Art Gallery will include a new Study Centre and improved on-site storage facilities, enabling greater access to the Costume and Textiles Collection in general. Lamentable at present is the inability to host larger conferences, though the construction of a new municipal library nearby will include the development of an existing building to include lecture facilities for joint use.

Although the Gallery has generally been very well received, one criticism has been over the loss of the romantic evening gowns of the 1930s and 1950s that had been a dominant feature of the previous gallery's display. One lady visitor, contemplating the "Renegade" case, was heard querulously to say: "But what happened to all those lovely costumes?" However, the curators responsible for the new gallery feel that the overwhelmingly enthusiastic and positive approach from large numbers of students, school children, younger and many older visitors fully endorses their decision to replace the ballgowns with brothel-creepers.

Acknowledgment

With thanks to Professor Lou Taylor for information about the historical background of fashion at Brighton and about the original gallery.

Note

Rebecca Quinton was recently appointed Curator of Costume and Textiles at Glasgow Museums. She has been replaced by Eleanor Thompson at Brighton.

Fashion Theory, Volume 8, Issue 3, pp. 351–354
Reprints available directly from the Publishers.
Photocopying permitted by licence only.

**Reviewed by
Valerie Wilson Trower**

Book Review

Through the Wardrobe: Women's Relationships with their Clothes Ali Guy, Eileen Green and Maura Banim (eds) (Berg, 2001)

When I mentioned that I was proposing to write this review, one well-known and well-published dress historian commented that she had not heard of any of the authors—mostly UK- or US-based sociologists. With two exceptions, I had to agree: perhaps demonstrating Lou Taylor's suggestion (Taylor 2002) that, despite our perceptions, the disciplines of dress, design history, and historical and critical studies interact in only a limited way with older social-science disciplines and vice versa.

The book is an example of a social-science methodology applied to subject matter which is often the focus of the study of other disciplines, for example, fashion and dress, historical and critical studies. In addition it seeks to explore the dialectic of "fashion as system" and "fashion as revealing identity." In order to do this, the book is divided into three sections: consuming images, constructing images, and personal images, with most of the chapters in the middle section falling in the "revealing identity" category. The editors question why selecting clothing is both a creative act of expression, and one that raises anxiety and dissatisfactions. They identify that strange phenomenon by which clothes become unflattering objects on being left in the wardrobe for some time, and conversely, ask how garments can be flattering on some occasions but not others.

The remit of the book is limited to the *fashion* dress (my italics) of ordinary women: these are defined as not employing professional stylists, and not, with the exception of Gillen's chapter on personal shoppers, having a professional fashion knowledge. A definition of fashion—in the chapters or in the introduction—would have contextualized the case studies reported, and a general understanding of the nature of fashion would have been helpful for all authors, for example: Abbott and Sapsford's chapter (p. 32) refers to "fashions that would not last" which must be an oxymoron. In the jointly written introduction (p. 7), Guy, Green, and Banim maintain that the fashion system caters only for women who conform to dominant discourses of femininity, observing that anything outside this narrow definition—by which I assume they mean the high street or shopping malls—is the remit of specialists, conveying the additional implied meaning that these are clothes "not wanted for bodies on display." Considering the entire fashion and clothing industry for a moment, we can see that this definition excludes some of the most desirable looks as well as the most mundane: from couture fashion to uniform and corporate dress (which Green's and Kaiser, Chandler, and Hammidi's chapters on academic dress touch on). It seems a pity that this definition is likely to have excluded work on mediation which would have employed methodologies familiar to social-science academics.

With the exception of Friese's chapter on the liminality signified by the wedding dress, the most interesting chapters are drawn from the last two sections. First, Tseëlon's critique of the shortcomings of social scientists' research methods and her own example is a pleasure to read. Secondly, Banin and Guy's work on why women keep clothes that they no longer choose to wear is interesting and a topic that I would have liked to have seen further developed: why do women recognize an obligation to, illogically, "wear out" fashion clothing? Cahill and Riley's chapter on body art is likely to be of great interest to fashion-studies students. However, the rather old-fashioned manner in which it is written is likely to limit its use to academics. Winn and Nutt's chapter on the stereotypes of lesbian dress would have benefited from the inclusion of images, especially as time will distance readers' memories of the garments that they describe. One of the most interesting chapters is that of Spense's examination of the role of a breast prosthesis in embodying society's fears in confronting possible, terminal illness and hastening a desire to return to "normality." This object-based case study raises further questions: namely, how fundamental is the bodily desire for symmetry?, as well as an examination of Spense's motives in using herself as a case study.

Without exception, the authors take great care to ground their contributions, citing appropriate preceding sociologists work while missing those of dress historians, the usefully combined bibliography at the end could have included the work of Carol Tulloch (Tulloch 1997–8, 1998, 1999), John T. Molloy (Molloy 1977), Paco Underhill (Underhill 1999), and others. A knowledge of the fashion industry at the editing stage would have precluded ill-informed speculation on the mechanics of the fashion industry—in several chapters—which weakens the strength of the work presented. In a parallel to Adam's chapter on imaginary shopping companions, I can hear the uniform chorus of "It's not like that," as I imagine fashion professionals reading this book. A more thoughtful editing would perhaps have excluded van Wersch's unhelpful chapter on breast reconstruction which generalizes from the specific.

Inevitably, female readers will find the research published here self-referential, which either lends conviction to the topics covered or suggests weakness, depending on one's view. The egalitarian decision to obviate price and cost information, with a few oblique exceptions has, in my view, also depleted the value of the research: we make a decision to purchase something based on merchandise, availability, fit, color, and price: why should this be investigated only partially when more detail would have been available when the data was collected?

To conclude, this otherwise interesting book rather falls between a number of stalls: not well enough informed for use in fashion retailing/marketing studies, too broad a scope for comparative literature–fashion studies, too sociologically focused for fashion-as-consumption studies but that said, I would recommend reading most of the chapters if only to increase one's understanding of fashion as seen through the eyes of sociologists.

Lastly, the book includes a rather whimsical (or ironic) profile of each contributor; as a reviewer of the book here is mine: An ex-accessories designer with a retail background, I currently work in the Fashion Retailing section of one of Hong Kong's universities and lecture in Design History in another. A complete fashionista, I wore Comme des Garçons and vintage clothing at my wedding, I am an "involuntary expert" (Christopher Reeve's words) on breast cancer, my hair is cut on a "Number 1" causing great confusion to lesbian women in London where I am also occasionally mistaken for a male.

References

Molloy, J.T. 1977. *The Woman's Dress for Success Book*. Chicago, IL: Follet Publishing Co.

Taylor, L. 2002. *The Study of Dress History*. Manchester: Manchester University Press.

Tulloch, C. 1997–8. "Fashioned in Black and White: Women's Dress in Jamaica, 1880–1907." *Things* 7, 29–53.

Tulloch, C. 1998. "Out of Many, One People: The Relativity of Dress, Race and Ethnicity to Jamaica." *Fashion Theory* 2(4), 359–80.

Tulloch, C. 1999. "That Little Magic Touch: The Headtie." In A. de la Haye and E. Wilson (eds) *Defining Dress: Dress as Object, Meaning and Identity*, pp. 63–78). Manchester: Manchester University Press.

Underhill, P. (1999). *Why we Buy: The Science of Shopping*. New York: Simon & Schuster.

Fashion Theory, Volume 8, Issue 3, pp. 355–358

**Reviewed by
Julia Pine**

Book Review

Fashion Classics from Carlyle to Barthes, Michael Carter (Berg, 2003)

Aside from the subject matter itself, perhaps the second most intriguing aspect of studying the history and theory of fashion is the spectacle of the creation of its own genealogy. Part of what seems to be the eruption of a discursive wellspring in the last decade, a number of notably self-reflexive works concerned, to varying degrees, with the historiography of fashion theory have been written, including Joanne Entwistle's *The Fashioned Body: Fashion Dress and Modern Social Theory* (Polity Press, 2000); Ulrich Lehmann's *Tigersprung: Fashion in Modernity* (MIT Press,

2000); and *Fashion Foundations: Early Writing on Fashion and Dress*, by Kim K. P. Johnson et al., eds (Berg, 2003). Dr Michael Carter, a senior lecturer in Art History and Theory at the University of Sydney, has just published what may be the most assertive of books in this genre to date, aptly entitled *Fashion Classics from Carlyle to Barthes*.

Unlike most other works based on critical approaches to dress, Carter's book has no problematic, such as modernity or subjectivity, through which he explores his theme. Instead, he singles out eight writers whom he considers seminal, and provides an in-depth exegesis of their respective fashion oeuvres. Each chapter covers one writer, including Victorian men of letters Thomas Carlyle and Herbert Spencer; American economist and sociologist Thorstein Veblen: anthropologist Alfred Kroeber; German sociologist and social philosopher Georg Simmel; John Flügel, a British advocate of Freudian psychoanalysis; British costume historian James Laver; and the French literary critic and theorist Roland Barthes.

Carter's approach is chronological and, according to his Preface, he has set out to document a progression of influence and intellectual exchange, resulting in what he calls the "Fashion Classics tradition." "The only novel feature that I can claim for this book," he writes, "is that it is the first time that a systematic study has been made of those figures, and texts, normally regarded as central to the study of clothing and fashion" (xi). In most cases Carter offers a short biography of each writer, and effectively situates each in their social and intellectual milieus before discussing their writings on the subject at hand. Although Carter singles out Spencer as a prime mover and claims his influence was felt by almost all subsequent writers he cites, the book is evenly paced, and I found his chapters on Simmel and Flügel particularly erudite and inspired. The chapter on Barthes also requires special mention. Like many people researching fashion, I had previously approached *The Fashion System* as a document concerned with dress, only to write it off as an impenetrable and rather obsessive semiotic exercise, in which Barthes had chosen clothing somewhat randomly, where it might have easily been substituted by food or furniture. Carter's careful inquiry into *The Fashion System*, in relation to works Barthes produced on fashion from 1956 onward, makes a strong case that Barthes was indeed interested in the modern fashion system, and that his dress-related output may well serve as valuable for the costume theorist, other than merely having codified the linguistic analogy prevalent in sartorial studies.

One reservation for this reader includes the diachronic narrative of the work. It seems to me that, as Carter is not always dealing with the same thing, the path of intellectual pollination he suggests is precarious. For instance, arguably Carlyle and Barthes were not writing about clothing *per se*, but using the concept of fashion primarily in a tropic sense: for Carlyle as a vehicle for social satire; for Barthes as a site for structural analysis. As such, perhaps they belong to a tradition other than that of Spencer, Veblen, Simmel, Kroeber, and Flügel, who were critical thinkers from various fields outside that of dress studies, looking at the phenomenology of fashion from the perspective of their respective disciplines. Also, Carter's decision to include Laver as the only costume historian seems to me exclusionary. Laver, by no means an academic, may have been the most prominent personality in the field of costume of the mid-twentieth century, but he was certainly not the only one, and surely the study of dress as a discrete discipline has its own ancestry apart from the theorists Carter enumerates.

From this point of view, Laver belongs to a different tradition, which begins much earlier with a number of possible writers, and is succeeded by more recent "big" names in costume, of varying academic intensity, such as Aileen Ribeiro, Lou Taylor, Richard Martin, Anne Hollander, etc. Selections of the work of these writers might be considered classics because they are easily as influential as Laver's and precede the above-mentioned discursive explosion on dress of the last few years in the domain of cultural and gender studies, visual culture, and what might be called "The New Fashion Theory." With all due respect to Carter's decision to end his "Classics Tradition" with the theoretical cachet of Barthes, Laver's inclusion easily could have paved the way for other costume scholars and "experts," and included works such as Elizabeth Wilson's *Adorned in Dreams: Fashion and Modernity* (Virago, 1985), or Valerie Steele's *Fashion and Eroticism* (Oxford University Press, 1985). Not only would these have provided a much-needed infusion of sexual and gender analysis to Carter's study (apart from cursory mentions and an extremely brief discussion in the chapter on Flügel), which primarily focuses on subjectivity, economics, and cultural relativity, they also would have added a female voice to the exclusively male canon Carter has charted.

Not to fault Carter for this line of inheritance. It is a fact that women were, for the most part, excluded from academic disciplines, for all the usual cultural reasons. However, *Fashion Classics* does, inadvertently, highlight the intensely gendered nature of the traditions of fashion writing. Unlike other scholarly fields previously dominated by the proverbial dead white European males, most notably history and art history, women were writing prolifically about fashion collaterally with men in the nineteenth and twentieth centuries, but, generally speaking, in the populist mode, through etiquette manuals, fashion journals, letters, novels, etc. As such, Carter's book highlights how truisms in the popular milieu were translated into the academic economy. In 1905, Simmel writes, "Judging from the ugly and repugnant things that are sometimes modern, it would seem as though fashion were desirous of exhibiting its power by getting us to adopt the most atrocious things for its sake alone" (78), a comment that could easily have been found in almost any turn-of-the-century women's journal, German or otherwise. Or how about Flügel's observation that,

> If we are to understand the motives that led to different kinds of clothing, to changes in our clothing and to the changes in our whole

attitude towards clothes, we shall have to be constantly on the look out for changes in the manifestations of these two fundamental conflicting tendencies, the one proudly to exhibit the body, the other modestly to hide it. (102)

Issues of revelation and concealment being, of course, in common parlance among fashionable women of almost any period.

Such reservations aside, however, I was thoroughly impressed by the territory *Fashion Classics* does cover, and highly recommend it to anyone with an interest in critical theory as it applies to dress and fashion. It smoothly and confidently fills a niche in published research, while making a surprisingly stimulating read. Perhaps Carter set himself up for minor criticism with his assertion that this was *the* "Fashion Classics" lineage, instead of simply one in a number of possible permutations. As such, as consumers and producers of fashion theory, it is worth keeping in mind that we are very much in the process of creating a genealogy, and keeping a close eye on the gendered, theoretical, and temporal strands we are drawing upon.

Fashion Theory, Volume 8, Issue 3, pp. 359-362
Reprints available directly from the Publishers.
Photocopying permitted by licence only.
© 2004 Berg. Printed in the United Kingdom.

**Reviewed by
Nicola White**

Book Review

Couture & Commerce: The Transatlantic Fashion Trade in the 1950s, Alexandra Palmer (UBC, 2001)

As Lou Taylor (1998) has emphasized in this journal, the study of dress history has been bedevilled by a division of approach between object-centered methods on one hand and socioeconomic history and cultural theory approaches on the other. Happily, although the divide still exists, the gap has been closing in recent years, perhaps most notably through the use of dynamic multidisciplinary research centered on the analysis of clothing consumption. Alexandra Palmer's book *Couture & Commerce: The Transatlantic Fashion Trade in the 1950s* makes an important contribution to this new generation of dress history research. It follows garments from European couture houses to the wardrobes of a number of elite Canadian women who selected and adapted couture to suit their own needs and tastes. The central aim is to assess the significance of *haute couture* in North America; this works against traditional couture history, which has tended to focus on eulogizing the designer as creative genius.

Luxuriously illustrated, the book offers an unprecedented insight into the complex mechanics of the *haute couture* sales system in the postwar years by following specific garments from Parisian design to sample to pattern (or toile) to copy/adaptation and finally to Canadian consumer. It gives a rare, detailed, and meticulously researched account of the private client experience of purchasing couture: how they purchased their couture, introductions, the role of the vendeuse, store buyers and staff as taste makers, and even the neglected role of the husband in this traditionally feminine sphere. Palmer's research into the archives of couture houses, the Royal Ontario Museum (Toronto) and private collections has unearthed a wealth of garments, drawings, and photographs with which to illustrate how they were altered, mended, worn (and worn), and even recycled, often over many years.

Palmer's methodology is clear and draws upon a wide range of primary sources; she combines garment analysis and archival evidence with interviews with those who sold, redesigned, and wore them, in order to debunk the mythology of *haute couture* exclusivity. As a case study there is a thorough and stimulating investigation of Canadian department store Holt Renfrew's licensing agreements with European couturiers, especially Christian Dior.

Palmer carefully maps out the minutiae of the symbiotic relationship between *haute couture* and the international fashion industry, which is fresh and significant in terms of our understanding of the history of *haute couture*, because it leads us to consider the broader context of fashion production. She argues that in terms of sales, publicity, and design development, trade buyers and press were vital to the continued success of the couture; even back in the 1950s, most profit was made in trade sales, rather than in unique made-to-measure garments for the individual. Palmer then investigates how Paris couture diversified into boutiques, *prêt-à-porter* collections, and licensed agreements with assorted manufacturers "in order to 'capture' the large numbers of affluent North American women eager to have Paris-inspired clothing" (p. 182). In doing so, she highlights the marketing problems of offsetting sales to mass-manufacturers against the maintenance of exclusivity.

We are shown exactly how department stores raised their style profile and their elitist status through their much-publicized retailing of Paris couture garments through publicity campaigns and in-store fashion shows, both public and private. These were, as Palmer states: "as influential as cultural marketing tools as they were as commercial devices" (p. 134). They promoted the store as arbiter of taste and their clients as leaders of Canadian style.

Central to Palmer's study is her astute scrutiny of the premise that European couture led the North American fashion market and that in turn, Paris dominated European couture. She explains how European couture was promoted by country of origin, but stresses through garment-based evidence that although Paris led in terms of status and price, Parisian couture was not always prized for design and function. She writes that among couture consumers in Toronto: "there was an implicit understanding that most French clothes were too extreme for Canadian tastes" (p. 96). Thus Palmer exposes for the first time the interwoven relationship between customer preference and couture retailing, a debate of very real interest in terms of both *haute-couture* mythology and issues of fashion identity. She shows us that couture style did not revolve entirely around designer dictatorship and further, that retailers and consumers shaped their own style. Palmer also demonstrates that this specific shaping was a direct result of the broader Canadian sociocultural context and this restrained sartorial taste.

Another first in terms of the chronicling of the history of Paris couture is that Palmer proves that there was a much wider distribution of couture and couture-related design than has previously been acknowledged. With Canada as a case study, the complex levels of couture reproduction are unpicked, from exact copies, to ready-to-wear mass-produced versions. There is a particularly intriguing analysis of the hitherto secretive retailing of the "bonded model," a disposable commodity which has been largely ignored by fashion historians. Bonded models were sold from couture house into America (especially the United States), but always remained within a customs bond in order to avoid the payment of import taxes (which could be as much as 90% of the garment cost) and they demonstrate clearly the breakdown of exclusive *haute-couture* merchandising. Garments were only rented for promotion and copying. Once out-of-date and of no value, they were sold off, out of their bonded status, often into Canada.

This process also illustrates the ways in which Paris couture design was altered to conform to local taste; this is not a new idea in itself, but Palmer gives it new impetus. Through an analysis of the ways that bonded and other models were pared down for reproduction, or rendered more modest in line with the more conservative Canadian taste, Palmer also explores the nuances of national taste and style. Significantly, she reveals that for many women, the copy or adaptation was as good as, if not better than, the original, because it was not only cheaper, but had also been re-engineered for their taste and lifestyle and still had cultural capital.

Clearly, high cost was only one aspect of the value of a couture garment; there were also sociocultural values placed upon it by the consumer. Palmer, again unusually within the history of books dealing with *haute couture*, analyses how a further series of sociocultural values were placed upon couture clothes by the consumer. It is extraordinary to learn that, according to Palmer's estimate, for the highest-income families in Toronto, spending on *haute couture* made up as much as 10–20% of family income.

Evidently, this was considered vital for the specific maintenance or enhancement of social status. Nonetheless, as Palmer states, in the late 1950s: "although couture retained its glamour and prestige, it was rapidly displaced . . . by copies and pret-a-porter" (p. 134).

Through her meticulous research, Palmer here explodes the myth of couture as "art" by focusing on its specific socioeconomic and cultural perspectives. She proves that "most Canadian couture consumers in the 1950s did not see their expensive dresses as passing luxuries but as long-term investments, that their Parisian garments were sometimes moderated to suit their Canadian tastes and that they purchased couture, above all, as a peer-group 'social uniform' and as a cultural requirement" (p. 354).

This is an important, well-researched, beautifully illustrated and clearly written book. Not only will it be invaluable to all with an interest in *haute couture*, but it also opens up major approaches in the new multidisciplinary dress history.

Reference

Taylor, Lou. 1998. "Doing the Laundry." *Fashion Theory* 2(4): 337–58.

Fashion Theory, Volume 8, Issue 1, pp. 363–366
Reprints available directly from the Publishers.
Photocopying permitted by licence only.

Book Review

**Reviewed by
Emma Tarlo**

***Dangerous Designs: Asian Women Fashion Diaspora
Economies*, Parminder Bhachu (Routledge, 2004)**

Fashions and fabrics with a South Asian resonance have in recent years
gained high levels of visibility in the contemporary global fashion scene,
whether in London, New York or Delhi. This book charts the biography
of a particular clothing form—the tunic, trouser, and scarf combination
known as salwar kamiz or Punjabi suit—and traces its transformation,
elaboration, and refashioning in the creative and entrepreneurial hands
of designers, marketers, boutique owners, and seamstresses of the South
Asian diaspora in London. Once negatively perceived as "ethnic dress"

with all the implications of marginality, backwardness, and timelessness associated, the salwar kamiz has, we are told, emerged as "a global garment, fashionable both on the margins and in the mainstream."

Parminder Bhachu seeks to understand and explain this elevation through an exploration of the hard work and creative zeal of second-generation British Asian women involved in the fashion industry. It is their improvisational diasporic aesthetic, their savvy exploitation of new technologies, their global connections, and local experience that have enabled them to create and market new hybrid fashions which, according to Bhachu, serve to redefine both British and Asian cultural identities as well as creating new commercial diasporic landscapes and economies. At the forefront of these developments are young entrepreneurial designers whose "dangerous designs" mirror their personal biographies as people whose lives do not fit the limiting cultural slots of East or West, Asian or British, but rather, whose lifestyles, politics, aesthetics have been forged through a complex reworking and fusion of cultural elements. At the same time, these experimental new designers owe much, we are told, to the less visible ground work performed by the first generation of immigrant mothers who stalwartly wore their salwar kamizes both in spite of and in defiance of racist hostilities and who kept alive a creative culture of *sina-prona* (needlework and related domestic activities) which they passed on to their daughters. This was particularly true in the case of twice-migrant women whose earlier dislocation from India to East Africa led them to develop and sustain their creative domestic skills in contrast to those women who migrated to Britain directly from India who had more access to the services of professional tailors. It is this history of double dislocation which, Bhachu suggests, gives multiply-migrant women and their offspring a certain creative diasporic edge over elite Indian and Pakistani fashion designers whose attempts to revive ancient skills, techniques, and designs are portrayed as purist, unimaginative, and out of touch with British Asian tastes.

The strength of the book lies in its ethnography of the domains of diaspora design, marketing, and stitching which is simultaneously an ethnography of the processes of globalization at work. A designer of British–African–Asian decent (Geeta Sarin) receives a phone call in her Wembley shop from a client living in, say, Trinidad. She already has the size and measurements of the client on her database. Details of color, design, material, style, and price are negotiated by phone. The designer creates a sketch with instructions which are faxed off to her production unit in India within the hour. Faxes are followed by phone calls to confirm the details and the finished outfit returns to Wembley via international courier service. The whole process from commission to the return of the finished product to London can be achieved, if necessary, within four days—demonstrating, as Bhachu says, the extraordinary levels of "time–speed–space compression" that define the globalization process. What links exclusive British Asian designers (whether they like it or not) to seamstresses working from their London homes is a cut and paste diaspora aesthetic which draws on a multiplicity of globally accessible design sources culled from Asian cable TV channels, Western and Asian fashion magazines, catalogs, film, and commercial sewing patterns as well as street fashions. This is not a universe of copyright or patent but a world in which ideas and designs are up for grabs and ripe for the copying, whether you are based in London, Delhi or Lahore.

Another striking feature brought out through the ethnography is the high degree of intimacy and localization enabled by the globalization process: a woman who migrated from London to Miami ten years ago retains the services of her "local tailor" in South London; a cloth merchant who migrated to London several decades ago can remember important events in the lives of his London-based clients from the days when they lived together in Nairobi; an importer of ready-made salwar kamizes who pops over to India every six weeks operates as some sort of commercial auntie in the British Asian fashion scene where she is endlessly invited to the weddings of a vast but highly personalized network of clients.

In contrast to many global business arenas, the South Asian diaspora fashion industry is a domain where women are at the center—as designers, entrepreneurs, importers, retailers, and consumers. Bhachu is convincing at demonstrating how they have created and co-opted a new commercial and aesthetic domain but her insistence that theirs is a form of "subaltern marketing," performed from a position of double marginality (as immigrants and as women) wears somewhat thin, unless one considers that gender and ethnic origins override such factors as economics and geographic location in what has become, in academic studies, a competition for subaltern status. What is clear, though never critically discussed by Bhachu, is that the entire South Asian diaspora design economy is built on the availability of cheap labor in Asian countries. One would like to know more of the other narratives that enable a garment to be designed in London, produced in India, and returned to London within a mere four days. It is not that one expects Bhachu to provide a detailed ethnographic study of production in India when this clearly is not her main field of study, but one does expect some engagement with the issue in a book that is essentially about the emergence and functioning of new global economies.

The incorporation of production within the theoretical framework of the text would not only create a more balanced global perspective, but would also shift the framework of analysis in significant ways. Viewed within this broader frame, successful London-based designers whose transnational clients are willing to spend hundreds, if not thousands, of pounds on a single outfit, slot uneasily into the category "subaltern." More obvious candidates might be the cutters, stitchers, buttonhole makers, embroiderers, weavers, dyers, and so forth in India. Similarly, the complex issue of the meaning of marginality needs to be interrogated rather than simply assumed. Throughout the book we are repeatedly told that British Asian designers are working "from the margins," but the margins of what and where? The discourse of margins is inextricably bound up with the discourse of centers, yet so much of Bhachu's ethnography, like other studies of the globalization process, demonstrates the multi-directional flow of ideas and goods that render the center/margins analysis theoretically problematic. This is not to say that the notion of margins should be abandoned altogether, but that it should be better explored and better contextualized. It is true that British Asian designers have always occupied (and to some extent, still do occupy) a marginal position in relation to the mainstream Western-dominated London fashion scene where they have had to work for inclusion against the tides of ethnocentrism and racism. But it is also true that in relation to the transnational South Asian fashion scene, British Asian designers and entrepreneurs located in London are extremely well placed. "We can use India and we can use the influence of people over there and get something different which no one else can do," says innovative designer Bubby Mahil, discussing the advantages of her ethnic background and contacts. Furthermore, London, with its thriving culturally hybrid music scene is widely acknowledged to be at the epicenter of diaspora fashion, in contrast to the more old-fashioned and provincial South Asian diaspora shopping centers found in New York, Los Angeles, and Toronto which, Bhachu tells us, resemble the shopping centers of London a decade earlier. Furthermore, ideas and designs from London have high currency back in India and Pakistan where they filter into factories and marketplaces, re-drawing the lines of the center/periphery equation yet again.

Questions remain concerning the extent to which the salwar kamiz and Asian fashion design more generally have "entered the mainstream" and redefined both British and Asian cultural identities in the process. One would need to know much more about the geography and sociopolitics of wearing to be able to assess this issue. At a recent conference on "gendering the South Asian diaspora," hosted jointly in London by the British Sociological Association Race and Ethnicity Group and Birkbeck College, there was not a single salwar kamiz in sight and only one sari in a room of just under a hundred people, the majority of whom were women of South Asian diaspora descent. Might this have been linked to cold weather conditions or are there other more socially and culturally meaningful explanations? Put more simply, who wears what, where, and in what context?

Dangerous Designs poses as many questions as it answers, but it remains a pioneering study of South Asian diaspora fashion, packed with fascinating material and insights that will be of interest to fashion scholars, cultural theorists, sociologists, and anthropologists.

Fashion Theory, Volume 8, Issue 3, pp. 367–370
Reprints available directly from the Publishers.
Photocopying permitted by licence only.

Book Review

**Reviewed by
Nicolas Cambridge**

**_Yeohlee: Work._ Edited by John Major and Yeohlee Teng.
Victoria: Peleus Press, 2003**

The black irregular shape that, on first glance, seems to be a jagged hole
torn in this book's pristine white dust jacket is, in fact, a photograph of
a figure swathed in a hooded cape; a talismanic item for Yeohlee Teng,
we are told—some version of which has appeared in every one of the
designer's collections since 1981. We also find out that she believes in the
power of numbers and in repetition, for the same design appears no fewer
than eight times in this volume—once for each of the essayists perhaps.
The fact that all the contributors have previous professional ties to Teng

suggests that the subtitle of the volume could refer not just to her creative output but also to the "intimate architecture" of relationships that exist between designer, journalist, critic and curator across the fashion cosmos. In the same way that certain images recur with mantra-like regularity, so the words of the contributors echo across the pages, each citing analyses made by the others. Consequently, the book resonates with their concerns for the uncanny—the totemic power of materials, clothing as a shelter for the soul, the fabrication of symbolic space, geometry and magic.

The term "magic" has previously been invoked by Pierre Bourdieu to describe how value is infused into clothing brands (Bourdieu 1975). His analysis involved the introduction of sportswear by Courrèges into a couture collection; here, by mystical coincidence, Teng is lauded for her innovative use of couture materials to create sportswear. It is the shared belief (Bourdieu calls it "collective misrecognition") in the magic by the players in the arena of cultural production that enables the voodoo of fashion to operate. Certainly, the author of this volume's introduction seems to have fallen under some kind of spell—how else could a fashion journalist refer the reader to a photograph with the caption "black wool doeskin," and in the next sentence describe the garment as "that khaki poplin cape"? Occult power operates through possession of personal items, and appropriation of Lou Luther's surname by the designer as title for a featureless gabardine jacket seems to have turned the garment into a fetish object for the writer.

Much of the enchantment of the designer's clothes derives from the manner of their display. Documentation of a series of exhibitions reveals shadowy, preternatural outlines, garments mounted on fractured torsos that float in mid-air, and clothes that retain a physical memory of previous wearers. Despite claims that the body animates Teng's clothes, curatorial decisions have rendered it invisible—as if the human form defiles the sacred aura of the designs. This is made explicit by Harold Koda, who voices an interpretation of her early output as "orchestrating a denial of the body" in a dialogue with Teng which occasionally demonstrates the gulf that exists between the respective disciplines. While the curator discerns the traditions of both tailoring and dressmaking in her work, for the designer this is a revelation. Conversely, attempts to unpack the design process are rebuffed with an unreflective "it was the most obvious solution." Similarly, the fascination that several of the writers evince for use of the selvedge as a design feature will leave most practitioners nonplussed, as will the enunciation of other standard creative techniques.

More rewarding is Andrew Bolton's discussion on the integration of construction and decoration in the designs, and their impact when shown in the transitional spaces of the Victoria and Albert Museum. He goes on to examine the use of pockets and seams as initiating factors, but juxtaposition of original design drawings against photographs of the outcomes (on pages 196–7) demonstrates the dangers of allowing geometry to dictate design. The aesthetically pleasing sketches for dresses featuring increasing numbers of pockets are not matched by the actual garments, because the platonic proportions that flow from the designer's pen are not achievable on the cutting table. Even the elegant models appear frumpy in the resulting sack-like shifts.

The photography is of a high standard throughout the book, and images from recent collections clearly indicate how the designer's work oscillates between the formal exercises that find favor with the design museums and the commercial applications of "high-performance" fabrics that appear in the collections. The monochrome fashion plates that freeze their couture-clad subjects into monumental grandeur are exquisite; less successful are pictures of models wading through the sartorial geometry on the catwalk or stepping gingerly down the staircase at the V&A. Contact sheets from one exhibition include an overexposure that bleaches the white portion of a dress into the background, leaving a dark, abstract form reminiscent of the images of Miyake's work produced by Irving Penn— giving credence to the suggestion by Richard Martin that the two designers share a rare integrity in their approach to flat-pattern cutting.

Thus the book provides a comprehensive introduction to a designer who has had limited exposure in the United Kingdom, and whose work falls into the spaces that lie between fashion, art, and costume. Visual documentation of the exhibitions spaces is enhanced by the inclusion of patterns, polaroids, posters and floor-plans. A coven of respected design theorists and critics supply written commentaries, but although these portray the designer in a variety of incarnations—Teng as architect, anthropologist, artist, atavist, costumier, dramaturge, and numerologist— the unstinting reverence for her work becomes rather cloying. A hagiographic undercurrent is perhaps inevitable given the limited critical distance between the essayists and their subject, but some contribution coming from outside the hermetic world of fashion curatorship might have also diluted the esoteric timbre of much of the writing.

Dorinne Kondo (1992) has noted the interpretation of designs by Comme des Garçons as a postmodernist deconstruction of high fashion, reflecting contemporaneous debates in academia. The valorization of Teng's work in this volume suggests that the designer may be thought to possess a similar 'currency' that can be cashed by those engaged in the project of advancing writing on fashion toward parity with that in other creative disciplines. It may be that the one-size-fits-all specification, utilized by Teng in the production of her ubiquitous cape, should have been employed for this volume in order to make it accessible to a more diverse readership. The text is quite severely tailored toward critical and theoretical understandings of fashion and display, but given the high-quality pictorial content, it should find a prominent place on any coffee table that has been designed using principles derived from sacred geometry.

References

Bourdieu, P. (1975), "Le couturier et sa griffe: contribution à une théorie de la magie", *Actes de la recherche en science socials*, 1: 7–36, cited by Skov, L. (2003), "Fashion-Nation", in Niessen, S. *et al.* (eds.) *Re-Orienting Fashion*, Oxford: Berg, pp. 215–242.

Kondo, D. (1992), "The Aesthetics and Politics of Japanese Identity in the Fashion Industry", in Tobin, J. (ed.), *Re-made in Japan: Everyday Life and Consumer Taste in a Changing Society*. New Haven CT and London: Yale University Press.

FASHIONFUTURES

Fashion Futures is looking for the best fashion students in Britain, taking fashion from college drawing boards to the catwalks of Paris as we select ten finalists to represent the UK in the prestigous Concours International des Jeunes Créateurs de Mode, the international competition for fashion students held yearly in Paris.

Visit our website to find out more about this year's competition. Be a part of Fashion Futures and join a creative forum that showcases designs from the leading young visionaries in Britain today.

www.fashionfutures.org

PFAFF

Design/ Bleed_Illustration/ Stina Wirsen